PRENTICE HALL
WRITING AND
GRAMMAR

Scoring Rubrics on Transparencies

Grade Eight

PEARSON

Prentice
Hall

Boston, Massachusetts,
Upper Saddle River, New Jersey

ISBN 0-13-361582-0

3 4 5 6 7 8 9 10   10 09 08

Practice Worth Repeating

**Activities, Puzzles, and Games
for Addition Facts**

 Creative Publications®

Acknowledgments

Writers Janet Pittock, Ann Roper

Editor Diane Nieker

Design Director Karen Lee

Design Gerta Sorensen

Cover Illustration Amanda Haley

Illustrators Sarah Frederking, Amanda Haley

Production Carlisle Communications, Ltd.

ISBN: 0-7622-1201-2

Catalog No. 32300

Customer Service 800-624-0822

http://www.creativepublications.com

3 4 5 6 7 8 ML 05 04 03 02 01

Contents

Introduction

Mastering addition facts provides children with basic tools that will help them achieve success in mathematics. This book provides efficient, motivating practice for memorizing those facts.

Overview

The prerequisites pages pinpoint key understandings that create a foundation upon which children can successfully learn basic facts. Use the information provided there to evaluate your children's readiness for the activities in this book. The prerequisites pages also offer some simple activities to develop readiness along with resource suggestions for additional activities if your children require further preparation.

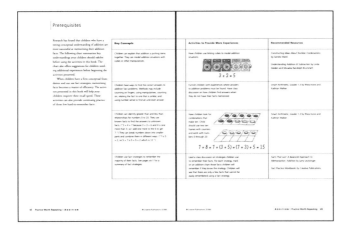

notes An addition fact test is provided in the first activity of this book, pages 2-4. Use this test to identify the specific addition facts each student needs to practice.

The activities that follow will help children focus on and improve their recall of the facts that have been identified. These activities can be used over and over again, even with the same students.

Whole Class Activity

●

Small Group Activity

●●●

Individual Practice Activity

●

Fact Strategy Summary pages list addition fact strategies children often use to learn their facts. Abbreviated information about each strategy is included.

There are three types of activities:

▶ Activities led by the teacher

▶ Activities for two to four children

▶ Activities in which children focus on specific sets of facts they need to practice. Many of the individual practice activities can be used as homework.

Prerequisites

Research has found that children who have a strong conceptual understanding of addition are more successful at memorizing their addition facts. The following chart summarizes key understandings your children should exhibit before using the activities in this book. The chart also offers suggestions for children needing additional experiences before beginning the activities presented.

When children have a firm conceptual foundation and can use fact strategies, memorizing facts becomes a matter of efficiency. The activities presented in this book will help your children improve their recall speed. These activities can also provide continuing practice of those few hard-to-remember facts.

Key Concepts

Children can explain that addition is putting items together. They can model addition situations with cubes or other manipulatives.

Children have ways to find the correct answers to addition fact problems. Methods may include counting on fingers, using manipulatives, counting on, relating the fact to one that is similar, and using number sense to find an unknown answer.

Children can identify greater than and less than relationships for numbers 0 to 20. They use known facts to find the answers to unknown facts. ("3 + 4 = 7 because 3 + 3 = 6 and 4 is one more than 3, so I add one more to the 6 to get 7.") They can break numbers down into smaller parts and combine them in different ways. ("7 is 5 + 2, so 5 + 7 is 5 + 5 + 2 which is 12.")

Children use fact strategies to remember the majority of their facts. See pages viii-1 for a summary of fact strategies.

Activities to Provide More Experiences	Recommended Resources
Have children use linking cubes to model addition situations.  $$3 + 2 = 5$$	*Constructing Ideas About Number Combinations* by Sandra Ward. *Understanding Addition & Subtraction* by Linda Holden and Micaelia Randolph Brummett.
Furnish children with experiences where answers to addition problems must be found. Have class discussion on how children find answers when they do not have their facts memorized.	*Smart Arithmetic, Grades 1-3* by Rhea Irvine and Kathryn Walker.
Using two ten-frames and counters, have children work with numbers 10–20, deconstructing one addend to make ten and left-overs. 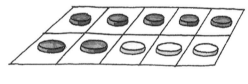 $$7 + 8 = 7 + (3 + 5) = (7 + 3) + 5 = 15$$	*Smart Arithmetic, Grades 1-3* by Rhea Irvine and Kathryn Walker.
Lead a class discussion on strategies children use to remember their facts. For each strategy, mark on an addition chart those facts children will remember if they know the strategy. Children will see that there are only a few facts that cannot be easily remembered using a fact strategy.	*Facts That Last: A Balanced Approach to Memorization: Addition* by Larry Leutzinger. *Practice Your Facts workbooks* by Creative Publications.

Fact Strategies Summary

Children often struggle to remember certain groups of facts. Help make the task of committing those facts to memory easier for your students. First, identify which facts each child needs to spend more time working on. Then, review strategies designed to help children learn those facts. A summary of the strategies follows.

+	0	1	2	3	4	5	6	7	8	9	10
0		1	2	3	4	5	6	7	8	9	10
1			3	4	5	6	7	8	9	10	11
2				5	6	7	8	9	10	11	12
3					7	8	9	10	11	12	13
4						9	10	11	12	13	14
5							11	12	13	14	15
6								13	14	15	16
7									15	16	17
8										17	18
9											19
10											

Commutative Property

The order of the addends does not affect the sum (4 + 7 = 7 + 4). Knowledge of the commutative property nearly halves the number of addition facts that children need to memorize.

+	0	1	2	3	4	5	6	7	8	9	10
0	0	1	2	3	4	5	6	7	8	9	10
1	1	2	3	4	5	6	7	8	9	10	11
2	2	3	4	5	6	7	8	9	10	11	12
3	3	4	5	6	7	8	9	10	11	12	13
4	4	5	6	7							
5	5	6	7	8							
6	6	7	8	9							
7	7	8	9	10							
8	8	9	10	11							
9	9	10	11	12							
10	10	11	12	13							

Count on

Counting on zero, one, two, or three is quick work. Children discover and use the simple rules for adding zero or one. Counting on twos and threes comes next. This strategy covers seventy-two (72) of the one hundred twenty-one (121) addition facts.

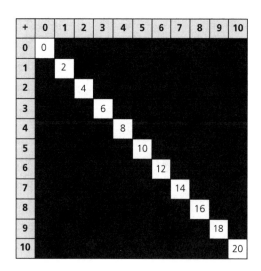

Doubles

Most children naturally remember doubles. Seeing pictures of doubles will help children remember these facts.

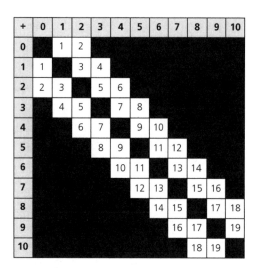

Near Doubles

Children combine knowledge of doubles facts with the count-on strategy. When children recognize that addends are only one or two numbers apart, they can find the double of the lesser addend and then count on to find the answer. Conversely, they can find the double of the greater addend and count back to the answer. There are thirty-eight (38) near doubles facts.

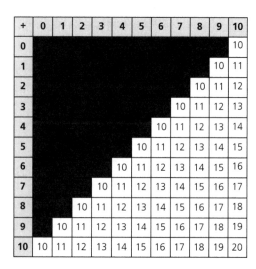

Using Ten

Several strategies relate to the structure of our base ten number system. These strategies include knowing pairs of addends that equal ten, adding ten to a single-digit addend, and decomposing an addend to create combinations that equal ten. $7 + 8 = (5 + 2) + 8 = 5 + (2 + 8) = 5 + 10 = 15$.

Activity 1 Finding Your Facts

Whole Class Activity

Description

Three 20- to 30-minute fact tests identify those addition facts each child has difficulty recalling. When choosing facts to practice in subsequent activities, children should focus on those they did not easily recall.

Materials

▶ Addition Chart, page 4, one (1) per child plus one (1) for teacher

▶ Fact Test, three (3) copies per child, plus (3) copies for use as a test key

▶ One hundred twenty-one (121) addition flashcards to include all combinations 0-20, separated into three sets

Time

Each test takes twenty (20) to thirty (30) minutes. You may want to spread the tests over a three-day period.

Allow five minutes for each child interview.

> **notes** Allow children only as much time as it takes you to write down the entire fact and answer. This will help to ascertain whether or not children have quick recall of facts.

Giving the Tests

❶ Give each child a copy of the fact test.

❷ Choose one of the three sets of flashcards. Show a fact to the class and read the fact aloud.

❸ Record each fact, including the answer, after the corresponding number on your paper after you read the fact to the class. Children should write only the answer. Your copy of the fact test will serve as your answer key.

❹ Show, say, and record the next fact. Follow this procedure through the set of flashcards.

❺ Repeat this process for the other two sets of flashcards.

Correcting the Tests

❶ Use the answer keys you created during each test. Write the complete fact (2 + 3 = 5) after each incorrect answer on the children's papers.

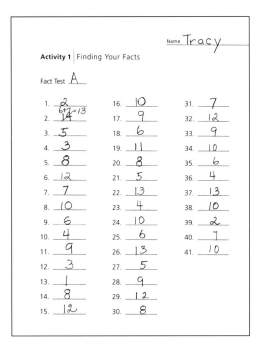

Name Tracy

Activity 1 | Finding Your Facts

Fact Test A

1. 2	16. 10	31. 7
2. 14 6+7=13	17. 9	32. 12
3. 5	18. 6	33. 9
4. 3	19. 11	34. 10
5. 8	20. 8	35. 6
6. 12	21. 5	36. 4
7. 7	22. 13	37. 13
8. 10	23. 4	38. 10
9. 6	24. 10	39. 2
10. 4	25. 6	40. 7
11. 9	26. 13	41. 10
12. 3	27. 5	
13. 1	28. 9	
14. 8	29. 12	
15. 12	30. 8	

❷ Prepare an addition chart for each child on which all facts the child missed are highlighted. As you do this, keep track of the most frequently missed facts so you can focus on them during whole class activities.

❸ After all three tests have been administered, checked, and individual addition charts have been prepared, meet with each child individually to discuss results.

❹ Children who have several facts to practice may need to gain more experience, or they may need additional practice in using fact strategies. For more information, see pages vi-1.

Activity 1 | Finding Your Facts

Fact Test _____

1. _____	16. _____	31. _____
2. _____	17. _____	32. _____
3. _____	18. _____	33. _____
4. _____	19. _____	34. _____
5. _____	20. _____	35. _____
6. _____	21. _____	36. _____
7. _____	22. _____	37. _____
8. _____	23. _____	38. _____
9. _____	24. _____	39. _____
10. _____	25. _____	40. _____
11. _____	26. _____	41. _____
12. _____	27. _____	
13. _____	28. _____	
14. _____	29. _____	
15. _____	30. _____	

Activity 1 Finding Your Facts

Addition Chart

+	0	1	2	3	4	5	6	7	8	9	10
0	0	1	2	3	4	5	6	7	8	9	10
1	1	2	3	4	5	6	7	8	9	10	11
2	2	3	4	5	6	7	8	9	10	11	12
3	3	4	5	6	7	8	9	10	11	12	13
4	4	5	6	7	8	9	10	11	12	13	14
5	5	6	7	8	9	10	11	12	13	14	15
6	6	7	8	9	10	11	12	13	14	15	16
7	7	8	9	10	11	12	13	14	15	16	17
8	8	9	10	11	12	13	14	15	16	17	18
9	9	10	11	12	13	14	15	16	17	18	19
10	10	11	12	13	14	15	16	17	18	19	20

Activity 2 | Addition Bingo

Whole Class
Activity

Description

Addition Bingo is a variation of the standard bingo game. Children create their own bingo cards by writing answers to addition facts in the squares on their cards as you read facts aloud.

The first person to cover or mark five numbers in a row is the winner.

Materials

▶ Bingo Board, page 7, one per child

▶ Pencil or twenty-five (25) counters per child

▶ Addition Chart, page 5

Time

Each game takes about five minutes and can be repeated as often as desired.

Getting Ready to Play

Select twenty-five facts to read to your class. Mark those facts on your addition chart.

Have children prepare their own bingo boards as you read the pre-selected facts and answers aloud at random (4 + 7 = 11). As you read each fact, children write the answer in a square on their board. Encourage children to place the numbers randomly. Continue until all spaces are filled.

Playing the Game

❶ Read a fact but not the answer. Keep track of the facts you have read.

❷ Have children cover or mark answers on their boards. Allow children only a few seconds to find an answer, then go on to the next fact. When a child has covered five (5) numbers in a row, vertically, horizontally, or diagonally, he or she calls out BINGO!

❸ Verify the BINGO by rereading the facts and having the children call out the correct answers. If the BINGO was correct, have children clear their boards and play again. If it was not correct, continue the game until there is a winner.

Activity 2 | Addition Bingo

B	I	N	G	O

Activity 3 | Capture the Prize

● **Whole Class Activity**

Description
Capture the Prize, a variation of "Grab the Bacon," gives everyone a chance to practice one of his or her facts. During play children practice other facts, too.

Materials
A chalkboard eraser or a knotted rag to serve as the "prize."

Time
Each game can take about 15 minutes, however play can be extended as long as desired.

Getting Ready to Play

❶ Assign an addition fact to each child. Children should be paired and each child of the pair given a different fact, however, both facts should have the same sum. The two children should be assigned to opposing teams.

❷ This is a loud, lively game that requires space. If possible, use the playground or gym. A basketball court is the perfect place for this game.

❸ Form two teams. Have teams line up facing each other on opposite ends of the play area, about thirty (30) yards apart. Place the "prize" in the exact center of the play area. As children race back to their line after grabbing the prize, they must stay inside the designated area or lose the prize.

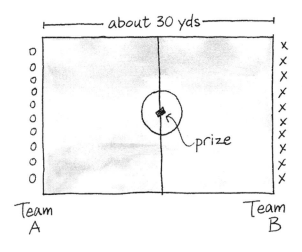

Playing the Game

1 Read a fact from your list. Do not read the answer. Keep track of the facts you have read.

2 All children who have been assigned the fact you read, plus all children whose fact has the same answer as the one read, run towards the prize. Each child tries to grab the prize and run back to his or her side without being tagged by a member of the opposing team.

3 A successful grab scores a point for that team.

4 Children return to their teams, and play continues with a new fact being called out.

5 The team with the greater score at the end of fifteen minutes of play wins.

Team A	Sum	Team B
✓ 6 + 7	13	5 + 8
4 + 9		4 + 9
✓ 9 + 5	14	✓ 9 + 5
7 + 8	15	9 + 6
✓ 8 + 7		✓ 8 + 7
	16	
	17	

notes The record of most frequently missed facts compiled in Activity 1 serves as an ideal list from which to draw when assigning facts to your students. Alternatively, have children supply facts they need to practice. Each child must find a partner who needs to practice a fact that has the same sum as his or hers. The two children join opposing teams. Having children set up their own teams in this manner can provide a problem-solving challenge for them.

Be sure to keep track of the facts your students supply. Their facts will make up the list of facts used to play the game.

Activity 4 | CrossNumber Game

Description

The CrossNumber Game is played very much like Scrabble.®

			3						
	5	+	2	=	7				
			4						
			=						
			7						

Materials

▶ CrossNumber Game Sheet, page 11

▶ A brown paper bag

▶ Paper and pencil for each player

Time

15 to 30 minutes

Getting Ready to Play

❶ Cut out the number squares and place them in the paper bag.

❷ Take turns pulling number squares from the bag until each player has drawn eight times. Write each number on your paper. Return the number square to the bag.

❸ Make sure other players do not see the numbers you write.

Playing the Game

❶ Make an addition fact using only numbers written on your paper. Cross each number off your paper as you use it. Use as many addition and equal signs as needed to make your fact.

❷ Write your fact on the game sheet. It can be written going across or up-and-down.

❸ Replace numbers you cross off your paper by drawing again from the bag.

❹ All new facts must be built on at least one number or symbol already on the game sheet. If you cannot play, you must pass. Trade in as many numbers as you wish by crossing them off your paper and drawing new numbers.

❺ The player with the greatest score wins. Your score is the sum of all the numbers you have placed on the board.

Activity 4 | CrossNumber Game

0	1	2	3	4	5	6	7	8	9	10
11	12	13	14	15	16	17	18	19	20	✂

Activity 5 | Fact Match

●●●
Small Group Activity

One (1) copy per group.

Description
Here is a chance to practice your facts and to show what a good memory you have, too. The better you know your facts, the better your chances to win.

Materials
Fact Match Game Cards, page 13

Time
5 to 10 minutes per game

Getting Ready to Play

❶ Make a list pairs of facts that have the same answer. Use the facts you need to practice.

❷ Cut apart the game cards. Write your fact pairs on the blank sides. Write one fact per card. Do not write the sum.

Playing the Game

❶ Mix the cards. Lay them face down in rows.

❷ Turn one card over. Try to make a match by turning over a second card that has a fact with the same sum. For example, 3 + 5 and 4 + 4 would match because they both equal 8.

❸ If you turn over two cards that match, keep both cards and take another turn. If your cards do not match, turn the cards back over. It is then the next player's turn.

❹ Play until all possible matches are made. The winner is the person with the most cards.

Activity 5 | Fact Match Game Cards

Activity 6 | Dragon Facts

●●●
Small Group Activity

One (1) copy per pair.

Description
Practice the facts you need to learn. Try not to get burned!

Materials
▶ Scratch paper and pencil

Time
Each game takes three to four minutes. All players should have the same number of turns drawing the dragon.

Playing the Game

❶ Write a fact on a piece of paper. Hide the paper from your partner.

❷ On a clean sheet of paper, write the fact putting blank lines where the numbers should be.

$$\underline{\quad} + \underline{\quad} = \underline{\qquad}$$

❸ Have your partner guess numbers to complete the fact. Use numbers 0 through 9. With four wrong guesses the dragon breathes fire and the game ends.

❹ As a missing number is guessed, write the number in the correct blank(s). If a wrong number is guessed, write that number in the corner of the paper and draw part of the dragon.

❺ Play again. This time have a different player write the fact.

Drawing the Dragon
For each wrong guess, draw part of the dragon.

Wrong guess 1 Draw the body.

Wrong guess 2 Draw the eye.

Wrong guess 3 Draw the teeth.

Wrong guess 4 Draw the fire and complete the dragon.

D1277450

EdThoughts

What We Know About Mathematics Teaching and Learning

edited by
Vicki Urquhart with
Carmon Anderson,
Linda Brannan,
Kathleen Dempsey,
and Matt Kuhn

Mid-continent Research for Education and Learning

ISBN 978-1-893476-13-8

The second edition of *EdThoughts: What We Know about Mathematics Teaching and Learning* was produced by a team of mathematics educators and writers from Mid-continent Research for Education and Learning with support from external reviewers from the faculty of Metro State College of Denver and Colorado Online Learning.

The first edition was a collaborative publication of McREL, the Association of State Supervisors of Mathematics, and the National Network of Eisenhower Regional Consortia and Clearinghouse. It was produced in whole or in part with funds from the U.S. Department of Education National Eisenhower Mathematics and Science Programs Office of Educational Research and Improvement (OERI), under grant R168R950025-00.

McREL
4601 DTC Boulevard, Suite 500
Denver, CO 80237
ph: 303. 337.0990, fax: 303.337.3005, e-mail: info@mcrel.org
www.mcrel.org

Contributors to the second edition

Writers and subject matter experts

Carmon Anderson
M.Ed., McREL

Kathleen Dempsey
M.Ed., McREL

Matt Kuhn
M.A., McREL

Reviewers

Ceri Dean
Ph.D., McREL

Brooke Evans
Ph.D., Metro State College of Denver

Don D. Gilmore
M.Ed., Metro State College of Denver

Jodi Holzman
B.S., Colorado Online Learning

Editor

Vicki Urquhart
M.Ed., McREL

Project manager

Linda Brannan
M.A., McREL

Librarian

Terry Young
B.A., McREL

Graphics and layout

Natalie Voltes
McREL

Jennifer Valentine
AQUENT

Cover art

Natalie Voltes
McREL

Indexing

Linda Brannan
M.A., McREL

Dear *EdThoughts* Reader,

Many good intentions have gone into ambitious education reform goals, including those ratified by the U.S. Congress in 1985. But the year 2000 deadline has passed, and our nation has not made measurable progress toward the goal of becoming "first in the world in mathematics and science education." In international comparisons, our students' overall mathematics and science achievement is mediocre. The Third International Mathematics and Science Study (TIMSS) from 1995 showed our 3rd- and 4th-graders scoring above the international average but our 12th-graders scoring well below. The TIMSS-Repeat results released in 2000 do not show significant improvement. In 2003, the Program for International Student Assessment (PISA) reported that 15 year olds' performance in mathematics literacy and problem solving ranked lower than the average performance for most industrialized countries. What can we do to make a difference?

EDThoughts provides a place to start. *EDThoughts* summarizes educational research and surveys of best classroom practices, and offers implications for improved teaching and learning. Classroom teachers and K–12 administrators will find this book useful for their own professional development; teacher educators can use it to inform and inspire their students, and parents and the public can read about the intended and achieved results of educational practices. Effective reforms in mathematics education practice and policy will require the collaboration of all of these stakeholder groups. They will need a common understanding of the current status of mathematics education and of the direction that Research and Ideas to Know About indicate for improvement as well as how they can help accomplish reform. We hope that this book provides a foundation for greater understanding and reflection.

Vicki Urquhart
M.Ed., McREL

Linda Brannan
M.A., McREL

Matt Kuhn
M.A., McREL

Carmon Anderson
M.Ed., McREL

Kathleen Dempsey
M.Ed., McREL

i

Table of Contents

Table of Contents

Preface to the second edition

As the way we live, work, and learn changes, ways of doing or communicating mathematics continue to emerge and evolve. The level of mathematics needed for thoughtful citizenship is increasing along with the need for greater mathematical problem solving. Today's students must develop skills to manage and use knowledge to solve problems in the personal, social, and economic realms, not just in textbooks. They need to know how to access, evaluate, and use information, all skills that are part of mathematics literacy.

Principles and Standards for School Mathematics (also known as the National Council of Teachers of Mathematics or NCTM Standards) published in 2000, describes a vision of a mathematically powerful student and offers a set of goals for mathematics instruction—the basic skills and understandings students need to function effectively in the twenty-first century. It asserts that enhanced career opportunities exist for those who understand and can do mathematics. It further states that mathematics education should prepare all students, not just a select few, to use mathematics appropriately in their careers and their lives.

The National Mathematics Advisory Panel was convened in 2006 to examine the best available scientific research to advise on improvements in the mathematics education of the nation's children. *Foundations for Success*, the Panel's final report lays out concrete steps that can be taken now toward significantly improved mathematics education, but it also views them only as a best start in a long process. The Panel's recommendations include a long range plan to improve the quality and quantity of research on effective mathematics education.

Our purpose in compiling this publication is to support reform of mathematics education and to bring to K–12 educators the rich world of educational research and practice. For each question we address, there is background information from the perspectives of research, followed by implications for improving classroom instruction. Each question concludes with a list of resources for further reading.

We recognize that the national mathematics standards and *Foundations for Success* describe not only important curricular content, but also ways to reform all parts of the educational system to promote improved teaching and student achievement. Systemic reform purposefully revises and aligns all components of a system. The mathematics education system is complex, including components such as assessment, curriculum, equity, student outcome standards, teaching, professional development of teachers, stakeholder involvement, leadership, and policy. While we don't address all of these topics in this publication, all are important in the context of systemic reform of mathematics education.

As classroom teachers are mainly concerned with what works in their own classrooms, *EDThoughts: What We Know About Mathematics Teaching and Learning* balances presenting research findings with drawing implications from it. The background research and related documents for the questions we include are intentionally succinct. There is, however, a full citation of all references in the back of the book. We encourage you to examine the primary source documents and to delve into educational research and apply the findings in your own classrooms.

Every person concerned with teaching and learning mathematics, whether teacher, administrator, student, parent, community member, or from the higher education community, will find useful information here. As the nation moves forward in reform of mathematics education, we must apply lessons learned to achieve improved mathematics education for all students—a goal we cannot afford to ignore.

Mathematics For All

All students can learn mathematics, and they deserve the opportunity to do so. The National Council of Teachers of Mathematics (NCTM) *Principles and Standards for School Mathematics (PSSM)* sets forth mathematics literacy expectations for all students and describes what all students are expected to learn. However, recognizing the diversity among our nation's children, educators do not expect all students to learn the material in the same manner, using the same resources, and in the same time frame. The Equity Principle in PSSM states:

All students, regardless of their personal characteristics, backgrounds, or physical challenges, must have opportunities to study—and support to learn—mathematics. Equity does not mean that every student should receive identical instruction; instead, it demands that reasonable and appropriate accommodations be made as needed to promote access and attainment for all students. (p.12)

To achieve "mathematics for all" will take a concerted effort from all stakeholders in our children's education. We must continue to make progress toward providing rich, well-supported learning environments that respond to the unique educational needs of every student. That is the goal of mathematics education reform.

What is equity and how is it evident in mathematics classrooms?

An equitable mathematics program provides high-quality mathematics education for all students.

Research and Ideas to Know About

An equitable mathematics program provides high-quality mathematics education for all students, where students not only have access to quality mathematics courses and instruction, but they also have the support they need to succeed in those courses. Equitable school programs must ensure that student differences in achievement are not based on race, ethnicity, gender, or physical disability. Some research suggests that access to and success in higher mathematics leads to greater financial opportunities; therefore, it is becoming the next civil rights issue.

The number of English-language learners in classrooms nationwide is increasing, even in localities where there were no such students just a few years ago. The achievement gap for minority learners also continues to widen. In addition, the field of special education has moved steadily towards the goal of inclusive instruction for students with disabilities. Differences in mathematics achievement among various gender, income, and ethnic groups have been widely reported. However, the National Research Council did not find significant gender differences among male and female students who had taken the same mathematics coursework.

Achievement in higher level mathematics is a gatekeeper to success in higher education and in 21st century careers. Group achievement differences in mathematics are often attributable to enrollment patterns or instructional strategies. Low-socioeconomic status (SES) students and those of color are half as likely to enroll in higher level mathematics courses as high-SES white students. Low-SES students and those belonging to minority groups who took high school algebra and geometry attended college in percentages approximately equal to high-SES white students who had enrolled in the same high school courses. Research indicates that when low-income and minority students experience greater success in high school mathematics and science courses, the achievement gap between students of differing ethnic and socioeconomic groups diminishes.

Research findings indicate that younger and lower ability students can learn and employ the same strategies and skills for mathematical reasoning and thinking as those used by older and higher ability students. Since different students learn in different ways, equal treatment for all students does not guarantee equal success. Teachers and counselors need to facilitate equal access to algebra, geometry, and higher level mathematics courses.

Implications to Think About

To create an equitable classroom, teachers use a variety of strategies to reach all students with high-quality content. These strategies include

- Clearly identifying the knowledge students need to master.
- Addressing different student needs and learning styles.
- Encouraging active participation by all students.
- Challenging all students by communicating high expectations.
- Diagnosing where students are struggling to learn and providing appropriate instruction.
- Embedding a variety of assessment types throughout units of study.
- Engaging all students in higher order thinking skills (e.g., data analysis, synthesis of results, and evaluation of potential solutions).
- Helping students make meaningful connections among related mathematics concepts, across other disciplines (e.g., science, social studies) and everyday experiences.
- Using inclusive language in all classroom communication.
- Engaging parents in student learning.

Teachers need adequate knowledge of mathematics content and pedagogy to effectively address the needs of a diverse group of students. Teachers should regularly take advantage of professional development opportunities that are content-specific in order to enrich their content knowledge and to stay abreast of the latest teaching techniques.

The physical environment of the classroom should be interesting and inclusive for all students, with visible displays of student work and materials that show diverse groups of people involved in mathematics activities and careers. The context for instruction (e.g., small group, large group) should invite all students to participate regardless of their current achievement levels.

The focus of an equitable mathematics program must be on student outcomes. Teachers and principals are responsible for the achievement of all students, and consequences for lack of student success fall not only on students, but also on teachers, principals, the school, and the family.

Resources for Learning More

Campbell, P., & Kreinberg, N. (1998). Moving into the mainstream.

Evan, A., Gray, T., & Olchefske, J. (2006). The gateway to student success in mathematics and science.

Moses, R. P., & Cobb, C. E., Jr. (2001). Radical equations.

National Mathematics Advisory Panel. (2008). Foundations for success.

National Research Council. (1989). Everybody counts.

North Central Regional Educational Laboratory. (2005). Critial issue: Remembering the child.

National Council of Teachers of Mathematics. (2000). Principles and standards for school mathematics.

Payne, R. K. (2005). A framework for understanding poverty.

Quiroz, P. A., Secada, W. G. (2003). Responding to diversity.

Schoenfeld, A. H. (2002). Making mathematics work for all children.

Tennison, A. D. (2007). Promoting equity in mathematics.

For All

Teaching

Assessment

Curriculum

Technology

Learning

What are the impacts of ability grouping and tracking on student learning?

Research and Ideas to Know About

When addressing diverse students' needs, teachers should consider the implications of placing students in various ability groups or tracks for mathematics instruction. Research suggests that these practices do not provide the same educational experience for all students. Foremost, the student should be the reference point for addressing the complex issue of who should learn what mathematics and when.

Studies suggest that student expectations differ according to assigned ability groups or tracks. Students deemed less capable experience less depth and breadth in school mathematics. Indications are that the most experienced teachers are assigned to teach high-level classes, while teachers with the least experience and mathematical background are assigned to teach the lowest-performing students in mathematics. Studies also reveal crucial differences in the kinds of instruction offered in different tracks. Instruction in the lower tracks tends to be fragmented, often requiring mostly memorization of basic facts and algorithms and the completion of worksheets. Although some higher track classes share these traits, they are more likely to offer opportunities for making sense of mathematics, including discussion, writing, and applying mathematics to real-life situations.

Tracking and ability grouping rarely allow for upward movement when a student makes a developmental leap. Hence, a conflict exists between the structure of academic tracks or ability groups and the potential academic and intellectual growth of struggling students who may be late bloomers.

An alternative to homogeneous strategies of tracking or ability grouping is mixed ability or heterogeneous grouping for instruction. Heterogeneous instruction emphasizes a differentiated classroom approach, in which teachers diagnose student needs and design instruction based upon their understanding of mathematics content using a variety of instructional strategies that focus on essential concepts, principles, and skills. Inherent in this practice is the opportunity for all students to receive quality mathematics instruction. As the demand for a more mathematically literate society continues, schools need to respond to this challenge and provide meaningful mathematics to all of our students, all of the time.

> Students deemed less capable experience less depth and breadth in school mathematics.

Implications to Think About

To effectively teach students coming from a variety of previous mathematics learning experiences and successes, teachers should thoughtfully choose instructional strategies for working with de-tracked or heterogeneous groups. The teacher must believe that all students can learn, although in different ways and at different rates.

These instructional elements have been shown to be effective for mixed ability mathematics classes

- *A meaningful mathematics curriculum.* This means providing contexts that give facts meaning, teaching concepts that matter, and framing lessons as complex problems.
- *An emphasis on interactive endeavors that promote divergent thinking within a classroom.* Students need to construct knowledge with peers, including safe and regular opportunities to take risks, exchange ideas, and revise their understanding of mathematics.
- *Diversified instructional strategies that address the needs of all types of learners.* To embrace multiple intelligences is to present information in a variety of ways.
- *Assessment that is varied, ongoing, and embedded in instruction.* Performance assessments, a portfolio of growth and achievements, projects demonstrating the accompanying mathematics, and solving and reporting on complex problems in varied contexts will provide evidence of student learning.
- *Focused lesson planning* that, instead of emphasizing what the classroom teacher wants to teach, begins by understanding what students need to learn (outcomes) and assessing what they already know.

Employing these techniques will provide a rich classroom experience and an effective way to enhance the learning of mathematics for all students.

Resources for Learning More

Battista, M. T. (1994). Teacher beliefs and the reform movement in mathematics education.

Moses, R. P., & Cobb, C. E., Jr. (2001). Radical equations.

Oakes, J. (2005). Keeping track: How schools structure inequality.

Tennison, A. D. (2007). Promoting equity in mathematics.

Tomlinson, C. A. (1999). The differentiated classroom.

Tomlinson, C. A. (2003). Fulfilling the promise of the differentiated classroom.

Tomlinson, C. A., & McTighe, J. (2006). Integrating differentiated instruction and understanding by design.

For All

Teaching

Assessment

Curriculum

Technology

Learning

What can schools do to facilitate students' opportunity to learn mathematics?

Opportunity to learn is facilitated through classrooms where there is a focus on higher order thinking skills, problem solving, substantive conversation, and real world contexts.

Research and Ideas to Know About

A basic definition of opportunity to learn (OTL) is the provision of a variety of circumstances and conditions to promote learning. Teachers serve as the primary OTL gatekeeper. While school counselors and other staff play important roles in facilitating OTL, it is mainly the teacher who assures that opportunities exist.

OTL components include being able to take needed courses, a curriculum that meets content standards and is free of hidden bias, time to cover content during school hours, teachers capable of implementing content standards, adequate educational resources, respect for diversity, and ancillary services to meet the mental and social welfare needs of all students. Research indicates that developmentally appropriate instruction is not just a function of age or grade; rather, it depends on students' prior opportunities to learn. OTL also refers to the absence of barriers that prevent learning. Today, the NCLB Act of 2001 includes OTL in its accountability structure for schools and teachers as a vehicle for improved student achievement.

Learning is an active process that allows students the opportunity to construct understanding through empirical investigation and group interaction. OTL is facilitated through classrooms where there is a focus on higher order thinking skills, problem solving, substantive conversation, and real-world contexts. Such classrooms engage students in social and interactive mathematical inquiry accomplished through evidence-based discussion and reflection on learning.

OTL is enhanced by linking student learning to their social and cultural identity. The premise of culturally responsive curriculum and pedagogy is that a student becomes more engaged in mathematical content when that content is significant to cultural beliefs and values. Using a context that students recognize and incorporating a variety of role models amplifies students' confidence and comfort with the content. These strategies demonstrate that everyone can be successful in mathematics.

Teachers' attitudes and expectations can affect student achievement by increasing or decreasing students' effort and performance. By varying instruction, understanding the differences in needs and learning styles of individual students, and fostering discourse, teachers facilitate the development of learning communities and create a climate that improves student achievement.

Implications to Think About

Skilled and qualified teachers, school counselors, administrators, and education policymakers can convey high expectations and help raise students' self-esteem and performance. Administrators and policymakers can ensure that there are appropriately prepared teachers for all levels of instruction. Graduation requirements should reflect the importance of algebra, geometry, and higher mathematics in students' future careers. High school administrators can provide teachers adequate instructional time through appropriate class scheduling, and counselors who assign classes must have as a goal appropriate higher level mathematics coursework for all students. Elementary school administrators should emphasize the importance of allocating adequate daily instructional time for mathematics, as well.

A standards-based curriculum combined with the creative use of classroom strategies can provide a learning environment that both honors the mathematical strengths of all learners and nurtures students in areas where they are most challenged. By including mathematics content from a variety of cultures and personal experiences, teachers enhance the learning experience for all students. When instruction is anchored in the context of the learner's world, students are more likely to take ownership and determine direction for their own learning. Teachers, armed with OTL strategies, help students take responsibility for their own learning.

To foster good mathematics teaching and high student achievement, adequate resources for classroom instruction should be available to all students. For a rich variety of investigations, students should use mathematical and technological tools, such as manipulatives, calculators, and computers. Schools that support equal access to mathematics supplies, equipment, and instructional resources are more likely to produce a student population with higher mathematical literacy.

Resources for Learning More

Duschl, R. A., Schweingruber, H. A., & Shouse, A. W. (Eds.). (2007). Taking science to school.

Herman, J. L., & Abedi, J. (2004). Issues in assessing English language learners' opportunity to learn mathematics.

Kilpatrick, J. & Swafford, J. (2002). Helping children learn mathematics.

Lester, F. K. (Ed.). (2007). Second handbook of research on mathematics teaching and learning.

Marzano, R. J. (2003). What works in schools.

National Mathematics Advisory Panel. (2008). Report of the Task Group on Learning Processes.

North Central Regional Educational Laboratory. (2004). Connecting with the learner

Tomlinson, C. A. (2003). Fulfilling the promise of the differentiated classroom.

For All

Teaching

Assessment

Curriculum

Technology

Learning

How can different learning styles best be addressed?

When there is a significant unaddressed mismatch between teaching and learning styles, students can be inattentive, bored, or discouraged and often perform poorly.

Research and Ideas to Know About

Learning styles are collections of personal characteristics, strengths, and preferences describing how individuals acquire, store, and process information. Learning style factors include information processing modes, environmental and instructional preferences, cognitive capabilities, and personality features. Individuals might demonstrate a balance among the dimensions of a learning style, or they might show strengths and weaknesses that have implications for course success and eventually for career choice. Groups of students from different cultures might exhibit distinct average learning styles, but there are often such broad within-group variations that generalizations about learning styles and cultural background are not valid.

Learning styles not only influence how individuals learn, but also how they teach. Teachers often instruct in the same manner in which they were taught even if the teaching style does not support the learning style that most students prefer. Teachers who are aware of their own teaching styles are able to make better choices of instructional strategies that do not impede student learning. They can interpret students' questions, comments, and answers in the context of learning style variations.

It is important for students to know their own learning style strengths and weaknesses and to develop a set of learning strategies that allows them to use their strengths and compensate for their weaknesses. When students receive instruction in the use of various learning strategies, they become more efficient and effective in their studying and more likely to attribute success or failure to their own choices rather than to their innate ability. Teachers who have taught their students about learning styles find that students learn the material better because they are more aware of their thinking processes. Students who are conscious of learning style differences develop interpersonal communication skills critical to adult success. Some findings from longitudinal studies suggest that students who are aware of learning style differences are better able to apply knowledge, are more satisfied with instruction, and have enhanced self-confidence.

Implications to Think About

Learning style strengths and weaknesses can influence task success and overall achievement. Students should know personal learning strengths and be able to use their knowledge to compensate for weaknesses. Tools for assessing learning (and teaching) styles are available. They can provide clues, not labels, to personal styles; learning styles are preferences, not traits or abilities. Students need to learn strategies for coping with varied learning environments and how to modify or generalize strategies for novel situations. Strategy use includes knowledge about the strategy, when to use it, and how to tell if it worked.

When there is a significant unaddressed mismatch between teaching and learning styles, students can be inattentive, bored, or discouraged and often perform poorly. In response, teachers may become overly critical, misinterpret poor scores as low ability (which exacerbates the situation), or become discouraged with teaching. Therefore, teachers must know how to identify learning and teaching styles and how to teach students to use various learning strategies. They can use differentiated instruction that is varied enough to meet students' needs while respecting diversity. Choosing from among standards-based learning methods, tasks, products, and assessments benefits diverse learners.

If teachers teach exclusively in a student's less preferred style, the student's discomfort can interfere with learning. However, students benefit from experience with non-preferred learning styles. Preferred styles are not static, and skill development in non-preferred modes encourages mental dexterity. Learning in the early stages of a unit may be more efficient using a different style than later in the same unit. It is important that the teacher balance instructional methods so that all students are taught partly in their preferred styles but also practice learning in less preferred modes. Teachers who vary their methods will be more effective than those who limit their instruction to one or two methods.

In assessing students whose learning will be demonstrated through different learning styles, a teacher should consider the criteria for success. Students may demonstrate learning in various ways, depending on learning styles, but in a standards-based classroom, the standards make clear the expectations for learning.

Resources for Learning More

Armstrong, T. (1994). Multiple intelligences in the classroom.

Burke, K., & Dunn, R. (2002). Teaching math effectively to elementary students.

Felder, R. (1996). Matters of style.

Gardner, H. T. (1993). Multiple intelligences.

McKeachie, W. (1995). Learning styles can become learning strategies.

Oberer, J. J. (2003, Spring). Effects of learning-style teaching on elementary students' behaviors, achievement, and attitudes.

Silver, H. F., Strong, R. W., & Perini, M. (2000). So each may learn.

Spoon, J., & Schell, J. (1998). Aligning student learning styles with instructor teaching styles.

Sprenger, M. (2003). Differentiation through learning styles and memory.

Teaching Mathematics

Learning and teaching mathematics are complex, active processes. Teachers constantly make decisions as they facilitate an environment in which students are active learners. They also must undertake long-term planning to connect daily efforts into the broader education of each student. At the same time, teachers share responsibility for their students' successes with other parts of the educational community, including their colleagues, their institutions, and the policies of the educational system.

The National Council of Teachers of Mathematics (NCTM) *Principles and Standards for School Mathematics (PSSM)* outlines theoretical and practical knowledge and understandings about mathematics, how children acquire mathematics content, and mathematics teaching techniques that facilitate each child's learning. Effective professional development moves teachers toward the goals spelled out in these professional standards for teaching mathematics. Because a teacher's classroom decisions affect the achievement of each student, teachers need to avail themselves of strategies that are as varied as their students and their educational needs.

What instructional methods support mathematical reasoning and problem solving?

Mathematical reasoning and problem solving requires teachers to teach mathematics as the power of thought rather than the power of discrete facts.

Research and Ideas to Know About

Research on best instructional methods for teaching and learning mathematical reasoning and problem solving consistently and clearly identifies the need for teachers to provide mathematically rich environments conducive to investigations.

Effective mathematics instruction occurs in community settings in which teachers carefully select problems, materials, and grouping practices, provide opportunity for mathematics discourse, and use assessment practices designed to provoke and support student thinking. Mathematical reasoning and problem solving requires teachers to teach mathematics as the power of thought rather than the power of discrete facts.

Instructional methods that support and promote student sharing and active listening enhance student reasoning and problem solving skills. Instructional practice should promote explorations supported by easy access to a wide variety of tools that are designed to accomplish a task. The tools students use influence the kinds of understandings they develop.

Both mathematics and science have standards of proof: an argument must be supported by evidence, and conclusions must be logically derived. Through questions and clarifications, teachers follow the evolution of student thinking in order to guide it effectively, and at appropriate times — but not prematurely — they introduce current ideas. Teachers who orchestrate the integration among conceptual, procedural, and factual knowledge provide the "sense making" that students need to develop confidence in their ability to reason and solve problems.

Implications to Think About

Classrooms that promote mathematical reasoning and problem solving typically are supportive, collegial communities. Teachers make instructional choices which support the opportunity for all children to learn important mathematics. Teachers find ways to support students as they work through challenging tasks without taking over the process of thinking for them, thus eliminating the challenge.

An effective classroom model includes a structure in which teachers pose interesting, challenging problems or tasks to the class as a whole. Time is allotted for students to

- Individually ponder appropriate strategies.
- Identify tools to assist in solving the problem.
- Work in small groups exploring and discussing ideas and solving the problem.
- Report their findings to the class.

Students are challenged to approach a problem by using logic and powers of observation, reasoning, models, evidence, examples, and counterexamples to discover meaningful patterns. Opportunities are provided for students who solved the problem differently to share their procedures, thus encouraging diverse thinking. Through classroom interactions, students develop mathematical ideas and conjectures and learn to evaluate their own thinking and that of others.

Effective instructional methods that promote mathematical reasoning include

- Comparing and clarifying.
- Analyzing information that leads to summarizing.
- Creating graphic representations, drawing pictures and pictographs.

Tools or manipulatives are integral resources for building understanding, but effective teachers recognize that the tools themselves do not provide meaning. Rather, they help students make connections.

Resources for Learning More

Bransford, J. D., Brown, A. L., & Cocking, R. R. (Eds.). (2000). How people learn.

Cawelti, G. (Ed.). (2004). Handbook of research on improving student achievement.

Hiebert, J., Carpenter, T. P., Fennema, E., et al. (1997). Making sense.

Marzano, R. J., Norford, J. S., Paynter, D. E., et al. (2001). A handbook for classroom instruction that works.

Marzano, R. J., Pickering, D., & Pollock, J. (2001). Classroom instruction that works.

National Council of Teachers of Mathematics. (2007). Mathematics teaching today.

National Council of Teachers of Mathematics. (2000). Principles and standards for school mathematics.

Pashler, H., Bain, P., Bottge, B., et al. (2007). Organizing instruction and study to improve student learning.

Thompson, C., & Zeuli, J. (1999). The frame and the tapestry.

How is mathematical thinking addressed in the mathematics classroom?

"Being able to reason is essential to understanding mathematics."

-National Council of Teachers of Mathematics (2000, p. 56)

Research and Ideas to Know About

Mathematical processes include problem solving, mathematical reasoning and proof, communication, connections, and representation. Mathematical thinking can help students acquire and use content knowledge and skills. It was once believed that the ability to solve mathematical problems automatically derived from knowing the mathematics. We now know that for all mathematical processes, students need a well organized understanding of the mathematics involved and experience solving a wide variety of problems. Simply put, students need many opportunities to use mathematical processes.

Reasoning and proof are mathematical processes that relate closely to scientific inquiry. In the process of proof, mathematicians often start by testing with numbers, then look at some special cases and test again. From this they can formulate a hypothesis and try to deduce the final result.

Mathematical reasoning also includes graphic and algebraic reasoning, proportional and probabilistic reasoning, and geometrical and statistical reasoning.

In the process of communicating their understanding of mathematics and trying to make their ideas understood, students amend and refine them. Communicating mathematics includes reading, writing, discourse, and using multiple representations. Definitions are important in mathematics, and students need to understand the role they play and use them in their mathematical work.

Connections among mathematical ideas help students build deeper understandings. Mathematics also connects with other subject areas and the real world, showing the power and practicality of mathematics. There are also connections between different ways that a mathematical idea can be represented.

Representations of mathematical ideas can be visual, such as equations, graphs, pictures, and charts. Representations may be in the mind of the student as he or she interprets the mathematical situation. Students can also use verbal descriptions and examples to communicate their ideas and findings. Students' mental representations of problems affect how they go about solving them. Students with well-developed understandings of a concept can represent it in a variety of ways.

Implications to Think About

Selecting worthwhile mathematical tasks that contain sound and significant mathematics is important. Tasks should be based on students' understandings, interests, and experiences and capitalize on the range of ways that diverse students learn mathematics. Teachers should choose tasks that require students to engage in mathematical thinking and problem solving, draw out students' thinking through effective questioning, and encourage reflection and sense making.

When selecting tasks, teachers should answer these questions

- Where will the task lead?
- Will students learn something new through engaging with the task?
- Does the task lead to model building?
- Does it lead to inquiry and justification?
- Does it involve flexible use of mathematical tools and technologies?
- Is the task relevant to the students?

Reasoning skills need to be continually developed through curricula that build on students' existing knowledge and also present ideas that demand new knowledge and understanding.

Connection of mathematical ideas promotes understanding so that students can apply that knowledge to learn new topics and to solve unfamiliar problems. Students develop understanding through the construction of relationships, by extending and applying mathematical knowledge, by reflecting about experiences, by articulating what they know, and by making mathematical knowledge pertinent to their own lives. All processes imply making connections.

Resources for Learning More

Driscoll, M. (1999). Fostering algebraic thinking.

Driscoll, M., DiMatteo, R.W., Nikula, J. & Egan, M. (2007). Fostering geometric thinking.

Fennema, E., & Romberg, T. A. (Eds.). (1999). Mathematics classrooms that promote understanding.

Hiebert, J., Carpenter, T. P., Fennema, E., et al. (1997). Making sense.

Hudson, P., & Miller, S. (2005). Designing and implementing mathematics instruction for students with diverse learning needs.

National Council of Teachers of Mathematics. (2007). Mathematics teaching today.

National Council of Teachers of Mathematics. (2000). Principles and standards for school mathematics.

Rigelman, N. (2007). Fostering mathematical thinking and problem solving.

Romberg, T., & Kaput, J. in Fennema, E. (1999). Mathematics worth teaching, mathematics worth understanding.

For All

Teaching

Assessment

Curriculum

Technology

Learning

What role does teacher questioning play in learning mathematics?

Effective teachers orchestrate productive discussions through purposefully prepared questions.

Research and Ideas to Know About

Teachers maximize learning when they encourage questions, expect students to elaborate on and explain their answers, and provide frequent feedback. In classrooms where there is effective instruction, both large and small group discussions between the teacher and students and among students commonly occur.

Effective mathematics teachers (those who are highly rated by their students and whose students perform well on both content and problem-solving skills assessments) ask well-planned questions of all types. Compared to less effective teachers, they pose more questions with higher cognitive demand, and ask more follow-up questions. Their students ask more questions, as well. Effective teachers orchestrate productive discussions through purposefully prepared questions.

Students in high-performing and conceptually oriented classrooms are expected to share ideas with others. Striving to explain their thinking helps students clarify their ideas, even when their thinking is not totally clear, or their understanding is not well formulated. Students who must explain their thinking organize their thoughts and analyze the strategies they used.

Studies of questioning in typical mathematics classrooms confirm that most questions make minimal demands on student thinking. Low-level questions do not give a good picture of a student's grasp of a concept. Low-level questions include yes/no questions; guessing; simple recall of fact, formula, or procedure; leading or rhetorical questions; and those answered immediately by the teacher. Answers often are immediately judged right or wrong by the teacher, and discussion moves to the next question. Increasing the wait time between posing a question and expecting an answer increases the number of responses, student confidence, responses by less able students, and reflective responses.

Implications to Think About

Better teacher questioning practices lead to better learning by all students. The foundation of good questioning is strong content knowledge, which is a critical factor in enabling teachers to understand and respond to students' questions. In addition, teachers must have a firm understanding of how students learn, so they can anticipate students' misunderstandings and plan appropriate questions.

Good questioning requires skill and planning. Strategies to improve questioning techniques include these

- Plan questions while preparing lessons. Write out questions to launch a lesson, and those to use during exploration.

- Choose different questions for varied purposes—clarifying, redirecting, summarizing, extension, open-ended, and reflection.

- Tape lessons occasionally to monitor levels of questioning.

- Focus questions on searching for student understanding; deemphasize right or wrong answers.

- Ask students to paraphrase what's been said. This improves attentiveness and assesses comprehension.

- Listen carefully to student responses, assuming that every answer is meaningful and "correct" to that student. The answers give insight into the student's mind and illuminate misunderstandings. They provide an opportunity for the teacher to learn about each student.

- Begin lessons with rich questions or problems to engage students and lead to new understanding of important content. Provide a variety of tools to assist mathematical exploration.

- Intentionally provide multiple opportunities for discussion and social interaction around mathematics ideas, thereby creating an environment conducive to high-quality mathematical discourse.

- Allocate time carefully. Make notes from class to class on effective amounts of time for each explanation.

- Increase wait time. An observant teaching partner can assist.

- Model self-questioning by "acting out" your thinking when you approach a problem. "I wonder what I should do next. Maybe I should try ___."

Resources for Learning More

Cawelti, G. (Ed.). (2004). Handbook of research on improving student achievement.

Hiebert, J., Carpenter, T. P., Fennema, E., et al. (1997). Making sense.

Johnson, J. (2000). Teaching and learning mathematics.

Kilpatrick, W., Martin, G., & Schifter, D. (Eds.). (2003). A research companion to principles and standards for school mathematics.

National Council of Teachers of Mathematics. (2007). Mathematics teaching today.

PBS TeacherLine. (n.d.). Developing mathematical thinking with effective questions.

Sullivan, P. & Lilburn, P. (2002). Good questions for math teaching.

Walsh, J. A., & Sattes, B. D. (2005). Quality questioning.

How can teachers motivate students to enjoy and want to learn mathematics?

Students will feel more capable in mathematics if they attribute success to their effort and if they feel their success is meaningful.

Research and Ideas to Know About

Students' perceptions of their performance in mathematics influence their motivation to learn. Student effort depends on expectations of success, whether the task is considered to be of value, and on whether the task was presented in an engaging way. The task must be challenging enough to compel attention but must offer a high likelihood of success given appropriate effort.

Teachers should encourage students to attribute their successes to diligence and perseverance and their lack of success to insufficient effort, confusion, or poor choice of strategy—not to lack of ability. Students will feel more capable in mathematics if they attribute success to their effort and if they feel their success is meaningful, than if they attribute success to ability, luck or external influences.

The classroom environment is important. Teachers' attitudes and actions greatly influence student motivation toward learning mathematics. More successful teachers are more knowledgeable about mathematics and are committed to the success of all students. Students need to engage in classroom discourse where they respectfully listen to, respond to, and question different ways of thinking. Students need to learn to make conjectures, to evaluate approaches and tools, to analyze strategies, and to present convincing arguments. An environment that allows for conceptual exploration and has space and tools for investigation helps students make sense of mathematics both independently and collaboratively.

Intrinsic motivation generally yields greater success than extrinsic incentives. Activities that build a rich understanding of mathematics increase intrinsic motivation; for many, there is nothing as exciting as learning. If students value mathematics, they become more skillful, achieve at a higher level, are more persistent problem solvers, and exhibit greater confidence. Additionally, extrinsic motivations such as grades and social pressure, when tied to student values, can also have positive effects. *Foundations for Success*, the final report of the National Mathematics Advisory Panel stresses the importance of effort on improved student performance in mathematics and encourages all educators to help students and parents understand the impact of effort on learning.

Interesting contexts stimulate learning and retention. Cooperative group interactions and social construction of knowledge contribute positively to student engagement and attainment. Multiple approaches allow students of different learning dispositions to gain access to problems, thus increasing motivation.

Implications to Think About

Awakening joy in learning is accomplished by creating a climate of choice, freedom from judgment, belief in each student's abilities, and knowledge that talent is expressed in many ways. Students need opportunities to satisfy their curiosities, test their imaginations, create, wonder, and invent. Classrooms that encourage playfulness, vitality, sensitivity, humor, and joy are inviting and stimulating. Environments that allow students to approach mathematics in many ways—with math tools, including manipulatives, technological tools, and hands-on activities—engage students' multiple intelligences.

Challenge and feedback are factors in maximizing brain growth. When students are challenged too much or too little, they give up or become bored. Many environmental factors provide challenge—time, materials, access, expectations, support, novelty, décor. Intellectual challenge is created through problem solving, critical thinking, relevant projects, and complex activities.

Opportunities to reflect allow learners to provide their own feedback. Teacher feedback influences students' motivations to do better work. Peer feedback that shows value and care makes learning more enjoyable and allows students to assess their ideas and behaviors. Feedback is most effective when it is specific, immediate, and gives the receiver explanation and a choice.

Emotion and attention are the processes our bodies use to survive and face challenges. We continually assess our internal and external environments to determine what's important. Emotion provides a quick, general assessment of the situation, while attention brings focus to the things that seem important. Curricular considerations related to thriving in an educational environment include

- Accepting and controlling our emotions (beliefs regarding mathematics).
- Using activities that provide emotional context (are more easily recalled and remembered).
- Avoiding emotional stress (self-esteem and mathematical confidence).
- Recognizing the relationship between emotions and health (an exciting atmosphere).
- Using metacognitive activities (talking about why a particular mathematical method was pursued).
- Using activities that promote social interaction (mathematics as a language).

Resources for Learning More

Armstrong, T. (1998). Awakening genius in the classroom.

Jensen, E. (1998). Teaching with the brain in mind.

Marzano, R. J., Pickering, D. J., & Pollock, J. E. (2001). Classroom instruction that works.

Middleton, J. A., & Spanias, P. (1999). Motivation for achievement in mathematics.

National Council of Teachers of Mathematics. (2007). Mathematics teaching today.

National Mathematics Advisory Panel. (2008). Foundations for success.

Sprenger, M. (1999). Learning and memory.

Sylwester, R. (1995). A celebration of neurons.

For All

Teaching

Assessment

Curriculum

Technology

Learning

What instructional strategies make mathematics more challenging and interesting to students?

"Almost all, who have ever fully understood arithmetic, have been obliged to learn it over again in their own way."

—Warren Colburn, educator & mathematician

Research and Ideas to Know About

The best instructional strategies respect the diversity of learners and use this diversity to enhance learning and achieve improved results. The American Psychological Association has developed research-based principles that focus more on psychological factors primarily internal to the learner but also acknowledge the interaction of external environmental factors with internal factors.

Among the cognitive and metacognitive factors are

- Learners link new information with existing knowledge.
- Learners use metacognition to select and monitor mental processes.

Among the motivational and affective factors is

- Teachers can influence motivation and effort toward learning.

Among developmental and social factors are

- Learning is most effective when it matches developmental readiness, specifically as it relates prior experiences and learning opportunities, rather than age, grade, or maturity level.
- Learning is a social activity.

Among individual differences factors is

- Learning is more effective when instruction takes diversity into account.

Effective teachers know their students well—their strengths and weaknesses, their interests and preferences—and plan instruction to challenge all learners to meet high standards. To do this, teachers must find ways to surface students' prior mathematics knowledge and understandings so that knowledge gaps can be addressed, inconsistencies resolved, and understandings deepened.

They must also learn about their students' backgrounds outside of school, so that mathematics instruction can be contextualized. Mathematics teachers must include development of metacognitive strategies and social and communication skills in their classroom goals. Effective teachers understand what students know and need to learn and then challenge and support them to learn it well.

Implications to Think About

One way students learn is by connecting new ideas to prior knowledge. Teachers must help students come to view mathematics not as an isolated set of rules to memorize, but as the connection of ideas, mathematical domains, and concepts. Effective instruction combines guided questioning with lessons that build upon the experiences and level of understanding that students already have. Strategies for accessing students' prior knowledge include K-W-L (What do you know? What do you want to know? What did you learn?), pre-tests, cueing and questioning, advance organizers, and journal writing.

Students benefit from time to reflect and gain a deep understanding of mathematics and to apply learned concepts and skills. As students struggle to solve problems, the role of the teacher becomes one of active listening, clarifying issues, and probing student thinking. When incorporating an inquiry approach to mathematical problem solving, questions teachers might ask include these: What would happen if? Can you solve it another way? What are you thinking? Tell me more about that. Why do you think that will work? Can you think of a counterexample?

Approaching a problem in various ways, making and testing conjectures, and justifying the reasonableness of various solutions are critical factors in the development of mathematical understanding. Effective instructional strategies engage students in interesting situations and meaningful problems that emphasize making sense of mathematical ideas.

Teachers should engage students in investigating a mathematical concept by posing an interesting and challenging problem that contains meaningful mathematical ideas and multiple potential pathways for reaching a solution. Students should use a variety of tools, including manipulative materials, calculators, Web-based resources, and interactive electronic devices to explore mathematics concepts and make sense of them. At times, students should work on problems collaboratively in order to share their strategies. Lastly, students should explain their mathematical reasoning, both orally and in writing, and have opportunities to write their own problems.

Resources for Learning More

American Psychological Association. (1997). Learner-centered psychological principles.

Colburn, W. (1821). Intellectual arithmetic, upon the inductive method of instruction.

Dowker, A. (1992). Computational strategies of professional mathematicians.

Heuser, D. (2000). Mathematics workshop: Mathematics class becomes learner centered.

Ma, L. (1999). Knowing and teaching elementary mathematics.

Marzano, R. J., Norford, J. S., Paynter, D. E., et al. (2001). A handbook for classroom instruction that works.

Marzano, R. J., Pickering, D. J., & Pollock, J. E. (2001). Classroom instruction that works.

National Mathematics Advisory Panel. (2008). Foundations for success.

For All

Teaching

Assessment

Curriculum

Technology

Learning

How does linking instruction and classroom assessment impact student learning?

Ongoing, embedded classroom assessment promotes student learning.

Research and Ideas to Know About

Classroom assessment, an essential tool for supporting and monitoring student progress toward mathematics standards, should be aligned with instruction. There is growing interest in formative classroom assessment, sometimes referred to as assessment for learning. Formative assessment is a systematic process of continuously gathering evidence about student learning. Teachers use the information they gather to adapt instruction to meet students' needs as learning occurs. Linking instruction and classroom assessment has at least three notable benefits.

First, classroom assessment embedded within a unit reveals to teachers what individuals and groups of students know, understand, and can do with the material they are learning. Embedded assessment may include informal measures such as observation, student interviews, and exit tickets or more formal measures such as student quizzes.

Second, ongoing, embedded classroom assessment promotes student learning. Classroom assessment should be accessible to students (i.e., asks them to use the skills and knowledge already mastered) and contain valuable mathematics content. Students whose teachers use open-ended assessment items have enhanced attitudes toward mathematics and perform better on high-stakes assessment items that are open-ended than do those whose teachers do not use them. According to the final report of the National Mathematics Advisory Panel, when teachers gather formative data and understand how to use the data to differentiate instruction, the effect on student learning can be significant.

Third, classroom assessment can help students monitor their own learning. When students know what is expected of them, through rubrics, feedback, and grading criteria, they are better able to keep track of their own mastery of the material. When students know the aspects of a skill or concept that will be assessed (e.g., written communication of their problem-solving strategy), they are more likely to meet the scoring criteria.

One research study showed that teachers who used open-ended, embedded assessments discovered the limitations in their own understanding of mathematical concepts. Another research study found that teachers who learned to incorporate open-ended assessment into their teaching were more likely to emphasize meaning and understanding, encourage students' autonomy and persistence, and instruct students in higher order cognitive strategies.

Implications to Think About

Assessment should be aligned with instruction that takes place during a unit. Using assessment data to inform instruction can make instruction more responsive to students' needs and ensure that every student gains the depth of knowledge and skill needed. Formative assessment informs teachers of student progress toward learning goals and allows them to modify instruction as needed to improve achievement. Noticeably, the teacher

- Embeds formative assessment in the learning process.
- Shares learning goals with students.
- Helps students know and recognize the standards.
- Provides feedback students can use to identify ways to improve.
- Commits to the idea that every student can improve.
- Reviews student performance and reflects with them on their progress.

Ongoing assessment may include informal conversations with and observations of students, open-ended problems that reveal students' understandings and misunderstandings, and traditional paper-and-pencil tests. Teachers should choose the type of assessment to use based upon learner and instructional needs. For example, knowing that students often omit finding common denominators in adding fractions aids instruction, whereas knowing that students can add fractions correctly is critical before moving on to the next topic. Teachers will not always have all the answers and need to be open to students' discoveries of novel approaches and unique understanding of the material.

Many types of assessment, including journaling and creating portfolios, involve student self-monitoring. Reflective self-assessment allows students to be more aware of their own learning and understand their strengths and weaknesses. This can improve communication of individual needs with the teacher, who can better understand student efforts and attitudes through examining the results of these self-assessments. Self-assessment thus serves a personal metacognitive goal of monitoring individual progress as well as a group goal of improving instruction.

Resources for Learning More

Black, P. (2003). Assessment for learning.

Fisher, D., Frey, N. (2007). Checking for understanding.

Gaddy, B. B., Dean, C. B., & Kendall, J. S. (2002). Noteworthy perspectives: Keeping the focus on learning.

Glatthorn, A. (1998). Performance assessment and standards-based curricula.

Heritage, M. (2007). Formative assessment.

McMillan, J. (Ed.). (2007). Formative classroom assessment.

National Mathematics Advisory Panel. (2008). Foundations for success.

Stepanek, J., & Jarrett, D. (1997). Assessment strategies to inform science and mathematics instruction.

Stiggins, R. (2005). From formative assessment to assessment for learning.

Svedkauskaite, A., & McNabb, M. (2005). Critical issue: Multiple dimensions of assessment that support student progress in science and mathematics.

For All

Teaching

Assessment

Curriculum

Technology

Learning

What impact does teacher content knowledge have on instruction?

Mathematics teachers with deep knowledge of mathematics content are able to teach rich mathematical content to all students.

Research and Ideas to Know About

Teachers need a deep understanding of the mathematics they teach—concepts, practices, principles, representations, and applications—to support effective instruction. A teacher's conceptual understanding of mathematics affects classroom instruction in a direct and positive way. Content knowledge influences the decisions teachers make about classroom instruction.

Differences between teachers who have a rich background in mathematics and those who do not are very evident in their teaching styles. When they possess explicit and well-integrated content knowledge, teachers feel free to teach dynamically with many representations of the same concept, and they encourage student comments and questions. Teachers with more limited content knowledge may depend too heavily on textbooks for explanations of mathematical principles. This often results in controlled classroom environments in which students work individually at seatwork, with mathematics portrayed as a set of static facts and procedures.

A close examination of mathematics teaching styles has revealed that teachers with less content knowledge more often emphasize algorithms and procedures. Although teachers with deeper content knowledge teach these same skills to students, they also engage them in forming a conceptual understanding of mathematics. When students understand the concepts of mathematics, they are better able to use mathematics successfully and demonstrate higher achievement on assessments.

Teachers should be familiar with common misunderstandings students have about mathematical concepts, such as confusing the least common multiple with the greatest common factor. Teachers' own mathematics knowledge should be deep enough to help them anticipate these misunderstandings. Teachers should use their knowledge of mathematics to clarify concepts during instruction and to recognize students' valid alternative problem-solving methods and solutions.

Implications to Think About

Secondary teachers of mathematics should have a degree in mathematics and be state certified, licensed, or both. All mathematics teachers should have a deep understanding of mathematics content. The NCLB Act addresses this concern with its requirement that all teachers be "highly qualified." Additional teacher preparation courses should focus on those pedagogical methods that are most effective for building mathematical concepts in children, such as teaching with mathematical and technological tools, allowing students to work collaboratively to solve problems, representing mathematics concepts in a variety of ways, and linking mathematics to other content areas.

Mathematics teachers with deep content knowledge are able to teach rich mathematical content to all students and analyze student work for evidence of conceptual misunderstandings. Content knowledge allows mathematics teachers to

- Present topics in the context in which they occur in daily life.
- Model content in a word problem format so students will become accustomed to the way mathematics is commonly encountered in the real world.
- Link mathematics to other content areas.
- Relate learning mathematics to an understanding of technology, personal and social perspectives, historical issues, and cultural values.

Skilled mathematics teachers use their knowledge to help students attain a deep understanding of mathematics concepts through activities with manipulatives and other mathematical tools. They encourage the strategic use of technological tools such as calculators and computers, so that students can spend more time working higher order problems. They also encourage students to participate in mathematical games. Teachers give students opportunities to use mathematics to answer real questions. They develop students' abilities to estimate and to evaluate the reasonableness of answers, thereby creating opportunities for sense making, which is essential for understanding.

Resources for Learning More

Ball, D.L, Lubienski, S. & Mewborn, D. (2001). Research on teaching mathematics.

Hill, H. C., Rowan, B., & Loewenberg Ball, D. (2005). Effects of teachers' mathematical knowledge for teaching on student achievement.

Kilpatrick, J., Swafford, J., & Findell, B. (Eds.). (2001). Adding it up.

Ma, L. (1999). Knowing and teaching elementary mathematics.

National Commission on Mathematics and Science Teaching for the 21st Century. (2000). Before it's too late.

National Council of Teachers of Mathematics. (2000). Principles and standards for school mathematics.

National Mathematics Advisory Panel. (2008). Foundations for success.

U.S. Department of Education. (2004, March). Fact sheet: New no child left behind flexibility.

What impact does teacher pedagogical knowledge have on instruction?

Despite significant changes throughout society over time, teaching methods in most mathematics classes have remained unchanged.

Research and Ideas to Know About

Pedagogical knowledge means understanding the methods and strategies of teaching. Specific methods or strategies that have been proven to work well in one content area, such as mathematics, are referred to as pedagogical content knowledge. According to the NCTM *Principles and Standards for School Mathematics,* "[e]ffective teaching requires knowing and understanding mathematics, students as learners, and pedagogical strategies." (p. 17)

Strong teacher content knowledge alone does not increase student knowledge, nor does the use of effective pedagogical methods without adequate content knowledge. In fact, rather than improve student achievement, it may actually reinforce student misconceptions. Despite significant changes throughout society over time, teaching methods in most mathematics classes have remained unchanged. Many students spend much of their time on basic computational skills rather than engaging in mathematically rich problem-solving experiences. The most direct route to improving mathematics achievement for all students is through different mathematics teaching.

Extensive research has focused on the influence of teacher characteristics (educational background, years of experience), professional development (training to support classroom practices), and classroom practices (small-group instruction, hands-on learning) on student achievement. Research shows that while all three components influence student achievement, the most influential factor is classroom practices. A principal message cited in the final report of the National Mathematics Advisory Panel indicates that instructional practice should be informed by high-quality research, professional judgment, and teacher experience.

Common mathematics teaching strategies, such as the use of worksheets and a heavy emphasis on computational fluency, are not as effective as engaging students in higher order thinking skills and hands-on learning activities. Professional development tailored to increase teacher repertoires of classroom instructional practices—coupled with knowledge of mathematics content—increases student academic performance.

Implications to Think About

Effective mathematics teachers employ a large repertoire of instructional methods, strategies, and models to produce more successful learners. Different instructional methods accomplish different learning goals for different students. Teachers should carefully select and plan classroom experiences to provide meaningful mathematics learning opportunities for their increasingly diverse student population. Highly effective mathematics teachers

- Have a deep knowledge of subject matter, which enables them to draw on that knowledge with flexibility.
- Encourage all students to learn for understanding.
- Foster healthy skepticism.
- Allow for, recognize, and build on differences in learning styles, multiple intelligences, and abilities.
- Carefully align curriculum, assessment, and high standards.
- Conduct interim assessments of students' progress and use the results to improve instruction.
- Measure instructional effectiveness through student performance and achievement
- Use a problem-solving approach.
- Hold high expectations for all students.

Teachers acquire and enhance their pedagogical skills through training, mentoring, collaborating with peers, and practice. To change the way they teach, mathematics teachers must receive first-hand opportunities to learn in different ways. They need to observe, practice, and refine high-quality teaching to master the art of teaching mathematics well. As teachers' pedagogical content knowledge increases within the context of a strong knowledge of mathematical content, their ability to have an impact on student learning also increases.

Resources for Learning More

Banilower, E. R., Boyd, S. E., Pasley, J. D., & Weiss, I. R. (2006). Lessons from a decade of mathematics and science reform.

Ma, L. (1999). Knowing and teaching elementary mathematics.

Marzano, R. J., Pickering, D. J., & Pollock, J. E. (2001). Classroom instruction that works.

National Commission on Mathematics and Science Teaching for the 21st Century. (2000). Before it's too late.

National Council of Teachers of Mathematics. (2000). Principles and standards for school mathematics.

National Council of Teachers of Mathematics. (2007). Mathematics teaching today.

National Mathematics Advisory Panel. (2008). Foundations for success.

Wenglinsky, H. (2000). How teaching matters.

For All

Teaching

Assessment

Curriculum

Technology

Learning

How do teacher attitudes about mathematics learning impact student achievement?

A teacher's attitude has a daily impact on the activities students will do and on student performance expectations.

Research and Ideas to Know About

Educational change depends on what teachers do and think, as does the success or failure of the educational process. Teachers mediate between the learner and the subject to be learned; consequently, teachers' beliefs, attitudes, and expectations have a major impact on student achievement. The study of teachers' instructional beliefs and attitudes, and their influence on instructional practice, has gained momentum over the past decade.

A teacher's attitude has a daily impact on the activities students will do and on student performance expectations. Teachers who believe it is important for students to learn mathematics with understanding embrace the use of investigations, mathematical discourse, and appropriate mathematical notation and vocabulary. Because a teacher's beliefs influence his or her instructional decisions, pedagogical choices differ among teachers, and varied student achievement results. A teacher's belief in a balance of whole class, individual work, and small-group work on challenging and interesting problems contributes to improved student achievement.

Teachers who believe in the importance of providing all students the opportunity to learn mathematics with understanding employ strategies that promote student engagement in problem solving. They encourage students to make, test, and revise conjectures, and to support their reasoning with evidence. In contrast, teachers who believe that computational prowess is the most important component of mathematics typically demonstrate procedures and provide students time in which to practice those steps. Students who experience a problem-solving approach to the teaching and learning of mathematics consistently outperform students in classrooms that focus on skills and procedures.

Implications to Think About

Teachers' decisions and actions in the classroom directly affect how students will learn mathematics. Teachers need to understand the big ideas of mathematics and be able to represent mathematics as a coherent and connected enterprise.

Student attitudes toward mathematics correlate strongly with their teacher's ability to help students clarify concepts and generate a sense of continuity between the mathematics topics in the curriculum. Effective mathematics teachers approach the content from a more holistic level of understanding. The development of students' positive attitudes in mathematics is directly linked to their participation in activities that involve both quality mathematics and classroom communication. Students who have positive interactions with their mathematics teachers tend to have high confidence in their ability to do mathematics. The attitude of the mathematics teacher is a critical ingredient in building an environment that promotes problem solving and makes students feel comfortable talking about mathematics.

While some mathematics teachers have beliefs that will positively affect their students' learning and achievement, others need to change their attitudes and expectations in order for their students to appreciate and understand mathematics. These teachers would benefit from professional development that starts with examining the impact of teacher beliefs, attitudes, and expectations on learning and achievement; includes a self-examination tool; and incorporates communities of practice for ongoing mentoring and support. Teachers' beliefs and practices change when they have opportunities to reflect upon innovative, reform-oriented curricula; their students' mathematical thinking; or aspects of their teaching.

Resources for Learning More

Fullan, M. G. (2001). The new meaning of educational change.

Handal, B. (2003). Teachers' mathematical beliefs.

National Council of Teachers of Mathematics. (2000). Principles and standards for school mathematics.

Philipp, R. A. (2007). Mathematics teachers' beliefs and affect.

Stigler, J. W., & Hiebert, J. (1999). The teaching gap.

What are the characteristics of effective professional development for mathematics?

"The quality of the outcomes for any school system is essentially the sum of the quality of the instruction that its teachers deliver."

–How the World's Best-Performing School Systems Come Out on Top (Barber & Mourshed, 2007)

Research and Ideas to Know About

Improving teacher quality is the key to increasing student learning. Teacher preparation must do more than transmit discrete skills and techniques to educators and then expect them to instruct students. Research clearly shows that effective professional development must be of adequate duration and must address subject matter and teaching methods.

A growing consensus about effective professional development is that it is most powerful when embedded in the daily work life of teachers to create a collaborative culture of inquiry about student understanding. In such an environment, teachers learn new content and related teaching practices, apply them in the classroom, and reflect on the results.

In this approach, dialogue about teaching and learning is guided by

- State and national standards that identify the most important content.
- Collected data about student learning (e.g., performance assessment, observations and interviews, standardized test results).
- Teachers' own inquiries about practice (e.g., action research, study groups).

As teachers build professional communities, they reduce professional isolation. The most effective schools have strong professional communities, characterized by ongoing collegial and collaborative inquiry into practice. Teaching improves in schools with cultures of collegiality, experimentation, and risk-taking.

In some districts, schools provide opportunities for expert, novice, and preservice teachers, university faculty, and teacher-leaders to collaboratively study teaching and learning. In such settings, school and university educators partner to improve classroom practices.

While the NCLB Act requires districts and schools to integrate professional development plans with their school improvement plans, it remains unclear as to the impact this approach has on student learning. Schools and districts that lack the capacity to apply knowledge about effective professional development may need additional assistance.

Implications to Think About

The five major purposes of professional development for teachers are (1) developing awareness, (2) building knowledge, (3) translating knowledge into practice, (4) practicing teaching, and (5) reflection. Different strategies address one or more of these different purposes

- Immersion in mathematics: engaging in solving mathematics problems as learners.
- Study groups: engaging in regular collaborative interactions around topics identified by the group to examine new information, reflect on classroom practice, and analyze data.
- Case discussions: discussing problems and issues illustrated in written narratives or videotapes of classroom events.
- Examining student work: looking at student products to understand their thinking in order to select the most appropriate instructional strategies and materials (Scoring assessments can lead to the same outcome).
- Action research: looking at one's own teaching and students' learning through descriptive reporting, purposeful conversation, collegial sharing, and critical reflection.
- Curriculum implementation: learning, using, and refining specific curriculum materials to build understanding.
- Curriculum development and adaptation: creating new instructional materials and strategies or adapting existing ones to better meet the learning needs of student.
- Coaching and mentoring: working regularly with another teacher at the same or greater level of expertise to improve teaching and learning.
- Lesson study: designing, implementing, testing, and improving one or several lessons over long periods, ranging from several months to a year.

In order to engage in this kind of professional development, policymakers at all levels need to support high-quality programs. In turn, teachers need administrator support, time to work with colleagues, and access to resources, such as research and outside expertise. For teacher learning and student learning to become a priority, the structure of schools and the policies affecting them must address professional development needs.

Resources for Learning More

Chicago Lesson Study Group. [Web site] http://www.lessonstudygroup.net/

Fernandez, C. Lesson study research group. [Web site]. http://www.tc.edu/lessonstudy/

Garet, M. S., Porter, A. C., Desimone, L., et al. (2001). What makes professional development effective?

Lester, F. K. (Ed.). (2007). Second handbook of research on mathematics teaching and learning.

Loucks-Horsley, S., Hewson, P. W., Love, N., et al. (Eds.). (1998). Designing professional development for teachers of science and mathematics.

Mewborn, D. S. (2003). Teachers, teacher knowledge, and their professional development.

Mid-continent Research for Education and Learning. (2005). McREL Insights: Professional development analysis.

Smith, M. S. (2001). Practice-based professional development for teachers of mathematics.

Sparks, D., & Hirsh, S. (1997). A new vision for staff development.

For All

Teaching

Assessment

Curriculum

Technology

Learning

Assessment in Mathematics

Assessment is a complex, systematic procedure for collecting and interpreting data and is the primary mechanism for feedback on the attainment of standards to students and teachers, parents, school districts, and communities. The National Council of Teachers of Mathematics recommends the use of multiple assessment methods. Since assessments communicate expectations, providing an operational definition of what is important, the NCTM *Principles and Standards for School Mathematics (PSSM)* promotes the inclusion of authentic assessments—exercises that closely approximate how mathematics is used in the real world.

The *PSSM* Assessment Principle also recommends measuring both student achievement and opportunity to learn. Interpreted together, this information assists educators and the community at large in assuring that all students can achieve to their potential. Opportunity to learn measures are important in interpreting both high-stakes individual assessments and international achievement comparisons.

What roles can assessment play in mathematics teaching and learning?

Student learning improves when appropriate assessment is a regular part of classroom practice.

Research and Ideas to Know About

With today's increased accountability for student learning, educators first think about testing as a way to gather feedback about how students are doing. This nationwide emphasis is solidified by NCLB, which requires states to provide report cards that include a host of statistics about school progress. State and other standardized tests provide data on overall school performance and can be valuable program evaluation tools. New approaches to mathematics teaching have expanded the role of assessment to include monitoring student progress and making instructional decisions. Essentially, assessment now plays four roles: 1) evaluate student achievement, 2) evaluate programs, 3) monitor student progress, and 4) make instructional decisions.

Student learning improves when appropriate assessment is a regular part of classroom practice. Using open-ended, inquiry-based problems is a teacher's best chance to assess a student's level of understanding. Research and professional mathematics organizations endorse the use of multiple and varied measures of assessment, such as performance-based assessment, teacher observations, interviews, student projects, portfolios, and presentations. Such alternative forms of assessment generate the information a teacher needs to determine what students are thinking, how they are reasoning, and what steps to take next. The National Mathematics Advisory Panel encourages and recommends regular use of formative assessment. The panel's report also indicates that formative assessment can be especially significant in improving student learning when the teacher understands how to incorporate the data to differentiate instruction.

National and state assessments have an influence on what teachers, administrators, and parents value in the classroom. These standardized, norm-referenced assessments tend to favor formats which give the impression there is always one right answer. Research supports that preparing students for such tests can have a positive effect on learning; however, such assessments typically provide only single scores or a small number of scores. Using them to make decisions about individual students is unwise. Educators should take care not to use standardized tests for wrong purposes. The most useful feedback about individual students comes from classroom assessments.

Implications to Think About

Assessment can help teachers plan curricula and guide daily instruction. An aligned curriculum has assessments that match what is being taught. Seamless instruction and assessment improves student learning.

Types of assessments include these

- Selected-response assessments (multiple choice, true-false, matching) best assess procedural knowledge and factual information. If well-constructed, they can assess complex understandings, but students cannot demonstrate all they know.
- Constructed-response assessments allow students to demonstrate their learning by choosing how to answer the question.
- Performance tasks integrate concepts, skills, facts, reasoning, and problem solving, but require extra time to implement and score.
- Observations, checklists, interviews, and portfolios allow students to show the depth of their understanding and can be especially appropriate for students who are English-language learners.
- Standardized, norm-referenced tests suggest students' relative strengths and weaknesses across different content strands.

Rubrics, used primarily with constructed response or performance assessments, describe levels of quality for the skills, knowledge, and understandings being assessed. Communicating these expectations to students prior to assigning tasks can promote quality work. Rubrics developed jointly by teachers and students focus learning on understanding, conceptual development, and problem solving.

Analyzing student work allows teachers see the depth of students' thinking and pinpoints sources of error or misunderstanding. Professional development that helps teachers analyze and respond to student work is important. Teachers need to become proficient in thoughtfully interpreting data from the various models of assessments (norm-referenced, criterion-referenced, and growth continuum). Learning to use evidence from multiple sources can yield a more accurate picture of what students know and are able to do. The data also can help educators ensure curricular alignment or determine whether to modify instruction.

Resources for Learning More

Blythe, T., Allen, D. & Powell, B. S. (1999). Looking together at student work.

Bright, G. W. & Joyner, J. N. (Eds.). (1998). Classroom assessment in mathematics.

Friedman, M. I., Harwell, D. H., & Schnepel, K. C. (2006). Effective instruction.

Gaddy, B. B., Dean, C. B., & Kendall, J. S. (2002). Noteworthy perspectives: Keeping the focus on learning.

National Council of Teachers of Mathematics. (1995). Assessment standards for school mathematics.

National Mathematics Advisory Panel. (2008). Foundations for success.

Olson, S. & Loucks-Horsley, S. (Eds.). (2000). Inquiry and the national science education standards.

Popham, W. J. (2007). Classroom assessment.

Stenmark, J. K. (1989). Assessment alternatives in mathematics.

Stiggins, R. (2004). Student-involved assessment FOR learning. Mathema

How can the use of varied assessments provide important evidence of learning?

The use of multiple types of assessments provides more "windows" into students' learning because students have more than one way to demonstrate their knowledge and skills.

Research and Ideas to Know About

Assessment should provide evidence about students' knowledge of mathematics. In order to do so, it must be congruent with state and local standards and be a good fit with the curriculum and instructional methods the teacher uses. As teachers strive to help their students achieve mathematical literacy (learning for understanding and the ability to mathematize problem situations), they need information about students' progress from a variety of sources.

Because different assessment strategies have individual strengths and weaknesses, using a wide variety of classroom assessments gives a better picture of student learning than any single approach. Multiple sources of evidence yield a more comprehensive, ongoing picture of student learning and academic progress and facilitate the exchange of information between teacher and students. They can be communicated readily to other members of the school community.

When their achievement is assessed by multiple means, students are more apt to assume greater responsibility for their input into the classroom discourse and become more reflective. They learn to listen more productively, communicate more clearly, and investigate more deeply. Using specific results to inform their actions, students gain confidence in tackling mathematics problems and in analyzing strategies and solutions.

The use of multiple types of assessments provides more "windows" into students' learning because students have more than one way to demonstrate their knowledge and skills. Multiple assessment measures, coupled with students' and teachers' awareness of the importance of assessment to teaching and learning for understanding, can help foster a learning environment centered on continual growth.

Implications to Think About

Mathematics teachers should discuss the importance of continuous assessment with students and provide scoring criteria and models of exemplary work to them before they begin a task. Some suggest that showing students models of partially completed work, or "anchor" papers that represent all levels of understanding and completion, fosters greater understanding of expectations, and therefore higher quality work. When students and teachers collaboratively establish assessment as a tool to inform classroom progress, finding a variety of measures becomes an important component of the instructional process. This includes making appropriate accommodations for students with special learning needs.

Effective teachers use questioning, classroom observations, interviews, and conferences to facilitate instruction and to inform decision making. Careful questioning helps students scaffold knowledge, focus thinking, and dig deeper into understandings. Observations framed around students' grasp of mathematics concepts, their dispositions toward learning, their communication abilities, and their group work contributions help the teacher identify appropriate instructional strategies. Interviews yield individual insights into a problem, a way of thinking, an orientation to problem solving, and a uniqueness of approach. Conferencing together, students and teachers can reflect on a student's learning and current disposition toward mathematics and set future goals. Conversation with peers also augments learning.

Individual self-evaluation through reflection (e.g., a mathematics autobiography, goal setting, daily evaluations, chronicling of "ah-ha's," record keeping, journaling) personalizes an activity for students. Through writing, in particular, students learn to organize, convey, question, conclude, and defend—these all are mathematics thinking processes.

The use of multiple means of assessment allows students to diversify their thinking and responses. Real-world problems, computer-based assessment, critical evaluation of mathematical logic, and structured problem-solving tasks stretch student thinking about meaningful mathematics assessment. Teachers need to increase their repertoire of assessment strategies and should have opportunities for ongoing professional development in which they examine an array of student work.

Resources for Learning More

Bush, W. S., & Greer, A. S. (1999). Mathematics assessment: A practical handbook for grades 9–12.

Bush, W. S., Leinwand, S., & Beck, P. (Eds.). (2000). Mathematics assessment: A practical handbook for grades 6–8.

Clarke, D. (1997). Constructive assessment in mathematics

Fennema, E., & Romberg, T. A. (Eds.). (1999). Mathematics classrooms that promote understanding.

Gaddy, B. B., Dean, C. B., & Kendall, J. S. (2002). Noteworthy perspectives: Keeping the focus on learning.

Glandfield, F., Bush, W.S., & Stenmark, J.K. (Eds.) (2003). Mathematics assessment: A practical handbook for grades K-2.

Stenmark, J.K., Bush, W.S., & Allen, C. (Eds.) (2001). Mathematics assessment: A practical handbook for grades 3-5.

Zemelman, S., Daniels, H., & Hyde, A. (1998). Best practice.

For All

Teaching

Assessment

Curriculum

Technology

Learning

How can mathematical thinking be assessed in the classroom?

In assessing applications and other problem-based contexts for doing mathematics, we need to be able to identify essential mathematics content that is embedded.

Research and Ideas to Know About

Perhaps you have heard mathematical thinking defined as "a search for truth or knowledge" or "a systematic investigation of a matter of interest" that embodies the mathematical processes of problem solving, inquiry, reasoning and proof, communication, connections, and representation. These processes are ways of acquiring and using content knowledge.

A task that is intended to assess mathematical processes should provide opportunities for students to tell about the mathematics they used, explain why they proceeded as they did, relate what they did to something they've done previously, and communicate their ideas in a manner most appropriate to them. For example, students might use pictures, graphs, discussions, written reports, or electronic displays.

Often, good instructional tasks also are effective assessment pieces. Assessment that enhances mathematics learning becomes a routine part of ongoing classroom activity rather than an interruption. Opportunities for informal assessment occur naturally in every lesson. Simple procedures like listening to students as they work, observing them, accumulating their work over time (portfolios), and interviewing them are some of the informal measures that can provide valuable information to students and to the teacher for instructional decision making.

Formal assessments often come in the form of performance tasks or student-constructed response items. Formal assessment items can be selected or created in ways that enable students to demonstrate what they know and can do rather than what they do not know. Performance tasks might include projects or investigations that students present to their classmates as presentations or displays. For example, students explore their neighborhood looking for a mathematics problem and then create a display of the problem and its solution. Or students could prepare a PowerPoint presentation on some aspect of the concept they just studied or a problem they liked.

Student constructed response items allow students to show their solution processes and explain their thinking. Rubrics, scoring guides, and quality examples should be shared with students in advance to communicate performance expectations. Effective scoring guides and rubrics give students credit for their insight about a task, their reasoning, the clarity of their communication, and the appropriateness of their representations, as well as for the accuracy of their results.

Implications to Think About

Assessing understanding requires multiple measures—both informal and formal—over time. Teachers need to use assessment techniques that measure students'

- Use of mathematics to make sense of complex situations.
- Work on extended investigations.
- Ability to formulate and refine hypotheses; collect and organize information; explain a concept orally or in writing; and work with poorly defined problems or problems with multiple answers, similar to those in real life.
- Use of mathematical processes in the context of many kinds of problems rather than in isolation.
- Understanding about mathematical concepts.
- Ability to define and formulate problems, question possible solutions, and look at all possibilities.
- Progress over time.

Since we are striving to assess higher order thinking, it is important to identify the components of the mathematical thinking processes. In assessing applications and other problem-based contexts for doing mathematics, we need to be able to identify essential mathematics content that is embedded, and we need to have some idea about how the context and content interact with performance.

Resources for Learning More

Bush, W. S., & Greer, A. S. (1999). Mathematics assessment: A practical handbook for grades 9–12.

Bush, W. S., Leinwand, S., & Beck, P. (Eds.). (2000). Mathematics assessment: A practical handbook for grades 6–8.

Clarke, D. (1997). Constructive assessment in mathematics.

Glandfield, F., Bush, W.S., & Stenmark, J.K. (Eds.) (2003). Mathematics assessment: A practical handbook for grades K-2.

Lazear, D. (2004). Higher order thinking.

National Council of Teachers of Mathematics. (1995). Assessment standards for school mathematics.

Shafer, M., & Romberg, T. A. (1999). Assessment in classrooms that promote understanding.

Stenmark, J.K., Bush, W.S., & Allen, C. (Eds.) (2001). Mathematics assessment: A practical handbook for grades 3-5.

Svedkauskaite, A., McNabb, M. (2005). Critical issue: Multiple dimensions of assessment that support student progress in science and mathematics.

For All

Teaching

Assessment

Curriculum

Technology

Learning

What do national and international assessments tell us about teaching and learning mathematics?

Mathematical competency is necessary for the changing economy and workplace, to prepare an educated citizenry for democracy, and for national security.

Research and Ideas to Know About

Results on national and international assessments provide a measure by which to compare U.S. student achievement in mathematics across states and nations. These results have forced mathematics educators, mathematicians, policy makers, and community members to examine the delivery system in PreK–12 mathematics education. Mathematical competency is necessary for the changing economy and workplace, to prepare an educated citizenry for democracy, and for national security.

The results of the Third International Mathematics and Science Study (TIMSS) showed that American students were not performing at acceptable levels in mathematics compared with their counterparts in other countries. Notably, 86 percent of eighth graders reported in the second TIMSS-R study (2001) that they worked from worksheets or textbooks on their own "almost always" or "pretty often" during mathematics lessons, which was higher than the international average of 59 percent. In 2003, The Program for International Student Assessment (PISA) reported that 15 year olds' performance in mathematics literacy and problem solving ranked lower than the average performance for most industrialized countries.

Concerns about performance on national and international assessments sparked the formation of the National Mathematics Advisory Panel in 2006. The panel's 20-month study focused primarily on school algebra and the preparation needed in grades PreK–8 to insure readiness for an authentic algebra course by grade 9. Released in 2008, the panel's main findings and recommendations addressed the areas of curricular content, learning processes, teachers and teacher education, instructional practices, instructional materials, assessment, and research policies and mechanisms.

Disaggregated NAEP results are instructive. Gender differences were statistically insignificant except at grade 12 where males outperformed females in mathematics. This difference can probably be attributed to the fact that males tend to complete advanced courses at a higher rate than females. Significant performance differences exist across ethnic groups at all grade levels even though the scores for each ethnic group have increased over the years. Factors such as socioeconomic status, home environment, and educational opportunities must be considered when interpreting the achievement differences among ethnic groups. The National Mathematics Advisory Panel recommends that NAEP and state assessments be improved in quality and emphasize the most important topics leading to algebra.

Implications to Think About

The national and state standards can be instructive to school districts as they develop local standards, documents, and procedures. The challenge is to limit the number of topics addressed without compromising the integrity of a demanding curriculum. Introduction of more complex topics earlier allows students to address gradually the underlying concepts of the rigorous content of algebra, geometry, discrete mathematics, and statistics. Attention to standards allows curriculum developers to create coherent, articulated curricular programs.

There is a connection between what is taught and how well it is taught. Student performance increases when students are taught to seek conceptual understanding rather than simply to follow procedures. Lesson design should reflect effective instructional strategies and should relate the various mathematical strands. Teachers, counselors, and parents should encourage students to continue their study of mathematics throughout high school.

International comparisons indicate that the most powerful instrument for change in student performance is improved teaching. A highly effective level of teaching

- Requires a deep knowledge of the mathematics being taught, as well as an understanding of what is most important to learn and what is most difficult to understand.
- Engages students not only in the computational aspects of mathematics, but also in its more meaningful conceptual aspects.
- Involves problem solving as students learn and apply the lesson content.
- Insists all students learn at high levels.
- Demands high quality professional development opportunities to keep teachers current in content, pedagogy, and assessment.
- Includes time to share with colleagues, which is critical in developing a learning community and professionalism among teachers.
- Uses the same kinds of mathematics tasks students in high-performing countries engage in.

Ongoing, planned professional development can enable teachers to achieve high levels of teaching. Designers of professional development for U.S. teachers could benefit from studying models used in other countries.

Resources for Learning More

Bush, W. S., & Greer, A. S. (1999). Mathematics assessment: A practical handbook for grades 9–12.

Institute of Education Sciences, (n.d.). Fast Facts.

National Center for Education Statistics. (2000). Pursuing excellence.

National Commission on Mathematics and Science Teaching for the 21st Century. (2000). Before it's too late.

National Council of Teachers of Mathematics. (2006). Curriculum focal points for pre-kindergarten through grade 8 mathematics.

National Mathematics Advisory Panel. (2008). Foundations for success.

Romagnano, L. (2006). Mathematics assessment literacy.

Schneider, M. (2007). NAEP–The nation's report card: Mathematics 2007.

Stigler, J. W. & Hiebert, J. (1999). The teaching gap.

Stigler, J. W. & Hiebert, J. (2004). Improving mathematics teaching.

For All

Teaching

Assessment

Curriculum

Technology

Learning

Mathematics *Curriculum*

The Content Standards in the National Council of Teachers of Mathematics (NCTM) *Principles and Standards for School Mathematics (PSSM)* define the content of instruction, outlining what every student should know and be able to do. It is the district curriculum, however, that describes how that content is organized. In addition, curriculum includes the emphases and perspectives placed on the content, creating a map for educators to use in designing classroom experiences for students.

Recognizing that the intent of content standards is to present a goal for all students, teachers must make curriculum decisions that accommodate a wide variety of learning styles, backgrounds, and interests. When educators use multiple means of addressing individual standards, all learners have an opportunity to access common content.

What is the importance of standards-based curricula in mathematics?

Standards are most visible in American classrooms as curriculum.

Research and Ideas to Know About

Standards are a set of expectations for what students will learn. Standards have grown increasingly pervasive during the last two decades. A standards-based curriculum arises from a given set of standards and provides the details of how students should progress through a variety of learning experiences in order to meet them. The Curriculum Principle of *Principles and Standards for School Mathematics* (PSSM) states, "A curriculum is more than a collection of activities: it must be coherent, focused on important mathematics, and well articulated across the grades." (p. 14)

Standards are most visible in American classrooms as curriculum. Standards-based mathematics curricula can increase students' understanding of mathematics, but programs must be implemented as they were designed. Taking the recommended amount of time to work through the scope and sequence, teachers should use all of the essential features of standards-based programs defined in the PSSM Curriculum Principle. These features include promoting classroom discourse, presenting mathematics skills in the context of problem solving, and applying learning to real-life situations.

Standards-based curricula and instructional guidelines can have positive influences on student achievement and can influence teachers to adopt research-informed instructional practices. Additionally, standards-based accountability systems and assessments exert strong influence on classroom instruction. Research shows that students who are at-risk of failing might receive less research-informed instruction but can benefit from it, provided access is assured.

Implications to Think About

Standards-based curricula are powerful means of implementing standards, but teachers who previously felt effective using traditional practices might need reassurance, coaching, and guidance during the implementation of a new standards-based curriculum. Programs that embed skill development in problem solving, games, real-world situations and other contexts are unfamiliar to many educators, and the path of skill development in such materials is not always obvious at a glance. Teachers need opportunities to experience sample lessons themselves and to try out multiple lessons while monitoring student learning.

Teachers who believe that skills are learned through repeated practice might be tempted to supplement a standards-based program with unrelated skills practice. Similarly, some teachers might be more comfortable with a direct instructional approach than with problem solving. Since one of the characteristics of standards-based learning is coherence, teachers should use the intended curriculum; otherwise, students are at an unintended disadvantage. Good curriculum materials have built-in teacher support.

Initial and ongoing professional development is crucial for teachers implementing standards-based curriculum. Students who have no opportunity to learn the content in standards cannot reach those standards. Administrators and policymakers must find ways to make instruction equitable among diverse groups of students if standards really mean high expectations for all students to learn. Classroom practice must provide avenues for all students to succeed in learning and using content materials.

Resources for Learning More

Hiebert, J. (1999). Relationship between research and the NCTM standards.

Hiebert, J., Carpenter, T. P., Fennema, E., et al. (1997). Making sense.

Hirsch, C. R. (2007). (Ed.) Perspectives on design and development of school mathematics curricula.

Mid-continent Research for Education and Learning. (2005). McREL Insights–Standards-based education.

National Council of Teachers of Mathematics. (2007). Mathematics teaching today.

National Council of Teachers of Mathematics. (2000). Principles and standards for school mathematics.

North Central Regional Educational Laboratory. (2005). Critical Issue: Mathematics education in the era of NCLB.

Schmidt, W., Houang, R., & Cogan, L. (2002, Summer). A coherent curriculum.

Senk, S. L., Thompson, D. R., (2003). Standards-based school mathematics curricula.

Sleeter, C. E., (2005.). Un-standardizing curriculum.

For All

Teaching

Assessment

Curriculum

Technology

Learning

How do we determine what students should know and be able to do in mathematics?

PSSM *identifies the "big ideas" in mathematics and how these concepts develop throughout the grade bands.*

Research and Ideas to Know About

There is a general consensus that mathematics is a "gatekeeper" discipline. Students who demonstrate proficiency in mathematics are more likely to take advanced courses in high school and to continue on to post-secondary education. NCLB requires states to set standards to achieve universal proficiency. The final report of the National Mathematics Advisory Panel provides further guidance regarding benchmarks for PreK–8 students and major topics of school algebra. The question of what mathematics all students should know and be able to do is, therefore, extremely significant.

It was this question that led to the development of the National Council of Teachers of Mathematics *Curriculum and Evaluation Standards for School Mathematics* in 1989 and its 2000 revision, *Principles and Standards for School Mathematics (PSSM)*. This question was further studied when the National Mathematics Advisory Panel was established by executive order in 2006. The standards in these documents and the recommendations from this panel reflect input received from mathematicians, mathematics educators, parents, business leaders, and teachers about what content and processes all students should know and be able to do to be mathematically literate and prepared for the 21st century workplace.

PSSM is not a traditional laundry list of topics similar to what you might see in the table of contents of mathematics texts; rather it identifies the "big ideas" in mathematics and how these concepts develop throughout the grade bands. The content areas in which all students must become proficient include: number and operations, algebra, geometry, measurement, and data analysis and probability. The process skills critical to achieving mathematics proficiency include: problem solving, reasoning and proof, communication, connections, and representation. Research indicates that when mathematics procedural skills are learned in the context of real-world content, students typically demonstrate a deeper understanding of mathematics than when those skills are practiced in isolation.

The standards also set an expectation that all students learn to value mathematics, become confident in their ability to do mathematics, become mathematical problem solvers, learn to communicate mathematically, and learn to reason mathematically. These mathematical habits of mind are applicable not only in using the content and procedures of mathematics, but in acting as a responsible citizen.

Implications to Think About

In a standards-based curriculum, teachers design learning experiences to enable all their students to reach the level of understanding or skill described by applicable standards. One area that demands more attention in mathematics is number sense—how numerical quantities are constructed and how they relate to each other. When instruction is rooted in daily experiences and connected to prior learning, students begin to think mathematically and to look for and analyze patterns in mathematics. Additionally, students need to make estimates, check the reasonableness of their answers, and demonstrate computational fluency in problem solving.

Learning geometry incorporates concrete models, drawings, and dynamic software. Studying measurement provides opportunities to learn about other areas of mathematics, including number operations, geometric ideas, statistical concepts, and notions of functions. Data analysis and probability are essential for informed citizenship. All students must formulate questions that can be addressed with data and have opportunities to collect, organize, and display relevant data to answer those questions. Students should use data analysis and probability to connect mathematics to other subject areas in meaningful rather than contrived ways.

Students should use multiple representations, choosing the appropriate representation for a particular problem. All students should be engaged in algebraic reasoning, not just manipulating symbols, but actively generating data; representing it in tables, charts, and/or graphs; identifying patterns and relationships; making predictions; and expressing relationships using symbols.

In order to maximize student learning, a balance of inquiry-based learning and direct-teacher instruction should be incorporated. Classroom experiences should promote the development of students' reasoning, justification, inquiry, and mathematics content skills. Students should be encouraged to use geometric representations for numeric and algebraic concepts, make and test conjectures, and be able to construct their own proofs.

Resources for Learning More

Collins, A. M. (2000). Yours is not to reason why, just plug in the numbers and multiply.

Grunow, J. E. (2001). Planning curriculum in mathematics.

Hirsch, C., Cox, D., Kasmar, L., Madden, S. & Moore, D. (2007). Some common themes and notable differences.

Kilpatrick, J., Swafford, J., & Findell, B. (Eds.). (2001). Adding it up.

Luft, P., Brown, C. M., & Sutherin, L. J. (2007, July) Are you and your students bored with the benchmarks?

Mokros, J., Russell, S. J., & Economopoulos, K. (1995). Beyond arithmetic.

National Council of Teachers of Mathematics. (1989). Curriculum and evaluation standards for school mathematics.

National Council of Teachers of Mathematics. (2000). Principles and standards for school mathematics.

National Mathematics Advisory Panel. (2008). Foundations for success.

Schoenfeld, A. H. (2004). The math wars.

What is curriculum coherence and articulation?

A coherent curriculum effectively organizes and integrates important mathematical ideas...Articulation ensures that there are connections.

Research and Ideas to Know About

Principles and Standards for School Mathematics (PSSM) states that a curriculum is more than a collection of activities; it must be coherent, focused on important mathematics, and well articulated across the grades. A coherent curriculum allows students to see how important mathematical ideas build on, or connect with other ideas, thus enabling them to develop new understandings and skills. An effective mathematics curriculum prepares students for continued study and for solving problems in a variety of settings.

Mathematics comprises interconnected topical strands that should be displayed prominently in the curriculum, instructional materials and lessons. Articulation describes the relationships among elements in a curriculum and ensures connections between lessons, units, courses, and grade levels. These connections support the increasingly rigorous development of ideas. A well-articulated curriculum challenges students to learn increasingly sophisticated mathematical ideas.

In national and international studies, the U.S. curriculum has been characterized as lacking in rigor, focus, and coherence. A comparison of textbooks and curriculum guides with those of other countries reveals that U.S. textbooks contain many more topics. Covering so many topics yields disjointed, rather than coherent, learning and does not allow students to develop a deep understanding of the topics covered.

High stakes assessment and accountability systems have prompted education leaders to identify important mathematics topics at each level. A review of grade-level learning expectations from state to state shows vast discrepancies in numbers of topic expectations at given levels. To help teachers and leaders make curricular decisions, NCTM released *Curriculum Focal Points for Pre-kindergarten through Grade 8 Mathematics* in 2006. Although PSSM remains the comprehensive document to identify concepts and skills across grade bands, *Focal Points* describes critical "targets" at each grade level and emphasizes the connections within and across mathematical strands.

In 2008, the release of the final report of the National Mathematics Advisory Panel commended *Focal Points* as a starting point for a more focused, coherent curriculum but called for even more reduction in topics. The panel recommends a PreK–8 curriculum which focuses primarily on preparation for algebra. It cites fluency with whole numbers and fractions and aspects of geometry and measurement as critical building blocks to success in algebra.

Implications to Think About

Several common practices contribute to a lack of coherence and articulation within a curriculum

- Emphasis on mastery, using re-teaching and repetition.
- Overuse of rote memorization.
- Content "coverage" by textbooks.
- Overly flexible, modular curriculum design which promotes inconsistent instruction.
- Lack of district attention to curriculum program development.

To achieve coherence and articulation, a curriculum program must

- Focus on the concepts and skills that are critical to understanding important mathematical processes and relationships.
- Help students develop an understanding of these concepts and skills over several years and in ways that are logical and recognize intellectual readiness.
- Establish explicit connections among the concepts and skills in ways that allow students to see and make those connections.
- Assess and diagnose what students understand to determine the next steps in instruction.

A coherent curriculum will typically contain fewer but richer topics that lead to greater depth and persistence of understanding. Content must be sequenced in a logical manner so that students accrue the experiences needed to develop understanding and see the relationships among ideas. A well-articulated, coherent curriculum should not only take advantage of important prior knowledge but also should have multiple entry points that allow all students who may have gaps in their prior knowledge to participate and learn rigorous mathematics content. Therefore, teachers must know what students need to learn in their current grade, what they learned in prior grades, and what they will need to be prepared to learn in future grades.

Resources for Learning More

Apthorp, H. S., Bodrova, E., Dean, C. B., et al. (2001). Noteworthy perspectives: Teaching to the core–Reading, writing, and mathematics.

National Council of Teachers of Mathematics. (2006). Curriculum focal points for pre-kindergarten through grade 8 mathematics.

National Council of Teachers of Mathematics. (2000). Principles and standards for school mathematics.

National Mathematics Advisory Panel. (2008). Foundations for success.

National Research Council. (1999). Designing mathematics or science curriculum programs.

Schmidt, W., & Valverde, G. (1998). Refocusing U.S. math and science education.

Schoenfeld, A. H. (2002). Making mathematics work for all children.

Stein, M.K., Remillard, J., & Smith, M. S. (2007). How curriculum influences student learning.

For All

Teaching

Assessment

Curriculum

Technology

Learning

What is the importance of reading and writing in the mathematics curriculum?

Reading and writing activities can help students analyze, interpret, and communicate mathematical ideas.

Research and Ideas to Know About

Reading, writing, and mathematics are, or should be, inseparable. Hands-on mathematics can stimulate curiosity, engage student interest, and build important prior knowledge before students read or write about the topic. The more students know about a topic, the better they comprehend and learn from reading more about it. Prior knowledge is the strongest predictor of student ability to make inferences from text.

Hands-on mathematics, though, must be combined with minds-on activities. Reading and writing activities can help students analyze, interpret, and communicate mathematical ideas. These are skills needed to evaluate sources of information and the validity of the information itself, a key competency for mathematically literate citizens.

Many of the process skills needed for mathematics are similar to reading skills, and when taught together, they reinforce each other. Examples of common skills are predicting, inferring, communicating, comparing and contrasting, and recognizing cause and effect relationships. Characteristics of mathematics texts that students find difficult include word density, direction reading (not only left to right, but also right to left, up and down, and diagonally), symbols, and mathematics-specific vocabulary. To address these, direct instruction is essential. Research continues to reveal that vocabulary knowledge is the single most important factor contributing to reading comprehension.

Teachers who recognize the interrelatedness of mathematics and literacy processes can design instruction that reflects these similarities. *Becoming a Nation of Readers* suggests that the most logical place for instruction in reading and thinking strategies is in the content areas rather than in separate lessons about reading.

The importance of writing in the mathematics classroom is paramount. During the writing process, students clarify their understanding of mathematics and hone their communication skills. They must organize their ideas and thoughts logically and structure their conclusions in a coherent way. Competency in writing can be accomplished only through active practice; solving mathematics problems is a natural vehicle for increasing students' writing competence.

Implications to Think About

Motivating and engaging students to speak, ask questions, learn new vocabulary, and write down their thoughts comes easily when they are curious, exploring, and engaged in their own mathematics inquiry. Teachers can take advantage of students' innate inquisitiveness to develop language skills while learning mathematics concepts. Integrating literacy activities into mathematics classes helps clarify concepts and can make mathematics more meaningful and interesting. Teachers can use a wide variety of reading sources, including trade books, texts, newspapers, technical manuals, Internet sources, and fiction. Selecting a fiction book with a mathematical theme both provides information and captivates student interest. Fiction works successfully with young learners by embedding cognitive learning in imaginative stories.

Asking students to write mathematics journals about their problem-solving experiences or to articulate and defend their views about mathematics-related issues provides opportunities to clarify their thinking and develop communications skills. Other ways to integrate writing in mathematics are recording and describing situations that involve mathematics, or writing persuasive letters on local or national issues that incorporate mathematics in their arguments like the use of sampling by the Census Bureau. NCTM provides annual lists of outstanding new literature and multimedia materials.

For English-language learners, mathematics instruction is enhanced when they can use hands-on materials to ask and answer questions or as visual aids in conversation with the teacher and peers. Teachers should provide visual and auditory clues, such as charts with pictures of materials and key procedures; select vocabulary carefully; repeat key words often; and refer to charts with the written words. Students should work in pairs or small groups to facilitate native language support by peers or instructional aides. Strategies that assist English-language learners also benefit all students.

Mathematics teachers can help all students increase their comprehension of mathematics texts by activating their prior knowledge through brainstorming, discussing the topic, asking questions, and providing analogies. Specific attention to content area vocabulary is essential to enable comprehension of mathematics texts. Simply looking up words in a dictionary does not promote real understanding. Teachers should introduce new vocabulary and use a graphic organizer, concept or semantic map, or collaborative peer study techniques to develop understanding of new words.

Resources for Learning More

Anderson, R. C., Hiebert, E. H., Scott, J. A., & Wilkinson, I. A. G. (1984). Becoming a nation of readers.

Barton, M. L., & Heidema, C. (2002). Teaching reading in mathematics.

Billmeyer, R., & Barton, M. L. (2002). Teaching reading in the content areas.

Buehl, D. (1998). Making math make sense.

Burns, M. (1995). Writing in math class.

Marzano, R. J. (2004). Building background knowledge for academic achievement.

Urquhart, V. A. & McIver, M. C. (2005). Teaching writing in the content areas. Teaching Assessment Curriculum Technology Learning

Wallace, F. H., Clark, K. K., & Cherry, M. L. (2006, September). How come? What if? So What? M

Wisconsin Department of Public Instruction. (2007). Mathematics: Adolescent learning toolkit.

For All

Teaching

Assessment

Curriculum

Technology

Learning

What are the most important considerations in selecting textbooks and other materials?

Because the quality of the instructional materials relates to student achievement, it is important to invest time and effort in materials selection.

Research and Ideas to Know About

Instructional materials for K–12 school mathematics include textbooks, manipulative sets, software, CDs, trade books, and other multimedia materials. They are a primary source of classroom mathematics learning as well as teacher professional development, which often is structured around these materials.

The process to select mathematics materials is critical to providing students and teachers with a solid foundation for improving achievement. Four key steps are 1) establishing a review/selection committee that includes teachers, 2) determining selection criteria, 3) selecting an evaluation instrument, and 4) evaluating and selecting materials. The process may be done at the district, school, department, or even the classroom level. Most decisions must be ratified by an administrator or school board. Many states review materials and restrict districts and schools to these approved materials.

An important selection criterion is that instructional materials develop the student understanding called for in the standards. Reviewers familiar with the discipline and the standards also should be familiar with what research says works. Quality instructional materials will

- Enhance student understanding.
- Promote students' active involvement.
- Hold high expectations for all students, with guidance for teaching diverse learners.
- Incorporate problem-solving skills.
- Use an appropriate learning sequence.
- Include assessment instruments and methods.
- Reflect current research in mathematics education.

Because the quality of the instructional materials relates to student achievement, it is important to invest time and effort in materials selection. Teachers also need professional development specific to using the materials. Finally, the effectiveness of the process and the selected materials should be evaluated before the next selection cycle.

Implications to Think About

Instructional materials that promote student learning in positive, innovative ways have strong mathematical content; are well-organized; contain content that relates to students' experiences and teachers' roles; and provide assessment suggestions. However, high-quality instructional materials alone cannot ensure that learning takes place. Teachers must appropriately use the materials in classroom activities and be knowledgeable about research-based materials. The What Works Clearinghouse is one resource that features scientific evidence of what works in education.

The mathematical content of the materials selected should reflect state or district mathematics standards. The organization of the program should include cohesive units, multi-day lessons, and worthwhile tasks that allow students sufficient time to explore and investigate ideas in-depth. Materials should develop understanding and abilities in mathematics and should clearly illustrate connections within mathematics and among other curriculum areas such as language arts, science, history, or art. Problem solving, communication, and reasoning should be built into the program at all levels.

Instructional materials should give students opportunities to be active, engaged learners, exploring and investigating mathematical ideas. Materials should ask students to communicate orally and in writing, with one another and with the teacher. Quality instructional materials provide suggestions to help students learn. The suggestions should elicit, engage, and challenge students' thinking, explain a variety of methods that give all students the opportunity to learn, and outline possible enriched or advanced work.

Student assessment should be integrated into the instructional program, using activities similar to learning activities. The materials should use multiple means of assessment and suggest ways to assess students individually or in small groups—through observations, oral and written work, student demonstrations or presentations, and student self-assessment. Conceptual understandings and procedural knowledge should be frequently assessed through tasks that ask students to apply mathematical knowledge in novel situations.

Resources for Learning More

Education Development Center, Inc. (2005). The K–12 mathematics curriculum center.

Goldsmith, L. T., Mark, J., & Kantrov, I. (2000). Choosing a standards-based mathematics curriculum.

Hellwig, S. J., Monroe, E. E., Jacobs, J. S. (2000, November). Making informed choices.

Institute of Education Sciences, What works clearinghouse. [Web site] http://ies.ed.gov/ncee/wwc/

Kulm, G., Roseman, J. E., Treistman, M. (1999). A benchmarks-based approach to textbook evaluation.

National Research Council. (1999). Designing mathematics or science curriculum programs.

North Central Regional Educational Laboratory. (2005). Critical Issue: Mathematics education in the era of NCLB.

Tarr, J., Reys, B., Barker, D. D., & Billstein, R. (2006, August). Selecting high-quality mathematics textbooks.

For All

Teaching

Assessment

Curriculum

Technology

Learning

In what ways can integrating curriculum enhance learning in mathematics?

Interconnections among the disciplines...support learning by making the mathematics curriculum more meaningful.

Research and Ideas to Know About

In real life, learning experiences are not separated into academic disciplines or subject areas. A student's classroom experiences should mirror this. Interconnections among the disciplines, when emphasized at all grade levels, will support learning and make the mathematics curriculum more meaningful.

Brain research has shown that long-term memory, or true learning, depends upon information that makes sense and has meaning. Subject integration helps a student make sense and understand the meaning of new information. Without these connections, students' learning experiences would add up to a collection of miscellaneous topics and unrelated facts. As early as 1938, John Dewey warned that isolation in all forms is to be avoided and we should strive for connectedness. *Benchmarks for Science Literacy*, from the American Association for the Advancement of Science, states that interconnected knowledge should be designed to "see the relationships among science, mathematics, and technology and between them and other human endeavors." (p. 320)

If the goal is to produce mathematically literate citizens who can apply mathematical thinking in real-life problem solving, then subject integration is essential. Problem-based learning using real-life problems is a powerful motivational tool. When connections extend across curriculum areas, they establish a mental framework that students can recall for future problem solving. This approach helps students see commonalities among diverse topics and reinforces understanding and meaning for future applications. Students can apply their newly gained knowledge to answer questions they have about why things happen in their world and discuss social implications.

The integration of subject areas often reveals interdependency among the disciplines. For example, to calculate the number of calories from fat eaten in a week and find daily caloric averages, you use both mathematics and science. Integrating subject areas also increases the chances of stimulating student motivation by connecting to an area of interest. An example of this might be connecting physics with physical education or sports, mathematics with music, literature with history, or botany with fine arts.

Implications to Think About

There are many models for integrating curriculum in the classroom. Curriculum integration may be designed and implemented by an individual classroom teacher or created by a collaborative team effort. Integrated or thematic units may be taught individually or by a multidisciplinary team of teachers, coordinating topics among otherwise separate departments. School culture often determines the most practical method for subject integration.

Mathematics can be effectively integrated at all grade levels with science, language arts, social studies, physical education, and fine arts, among other areas. Language arts (reading, writing, and communication) should be a strong component of all the disciplines. If the content is rigorous and relevant, debates, storytelling, art, music, drama, games, mnemonics, graphic organizers, and hands-on and "minds-on" laboratories can dramatically enhance student learning.

Mathematics and science are natural partners, sharing similar goals of building process and problem-solving skills. The integration of mathematics and science provides innovative projects that encourage students to learn. For example, asking students to build a weight-bearing bridge requires students to budget, do a cost analysis of their project, and conceptualize and communicate how their completed project will look before building it.

There are many avenues of integration between mathematics and social studies. History often revolves around great advances in mathematics, and a study of important mathematical ideas helps students conceptualize the concepts of mathematics and see how ideas change over time. Both societal and mathematical perspectives can provide learning opportunities.

The challenges to subject integration are lack of imagination, inadequate teacher training, hindrances to teacher collaboration, and insufficient materials. However, the benefits to the learning process should spur teachers beyond those limitations to develop quality, integrated curricula.

Resources for Learning More

American Association for the Advancement of Science, Project 2061. (1993). Benchmarks for science literacy.

Bailey, T. (1997). Integrating vocational and academic education.

Frykholm, J. A. (2005). Integrating mathematics and science.

Hoachlander, G. (1997). Organizing mathematics education around work.

Horton, R. M., Hedetniemi, T., Wiegert, E., & Wagner, J. R. (2006). Integrating curriculum through themes.

O'Donnell, B. D. (2001, April). A personal journey.

Seki, J. M", & Menon, R. (2007, February). Incorporating mathematics into the science program of students labeled "at-risk.

Sousa, D. A. (2005). How the brain learns.

Westwater, A., & Wolfe, P. (2000). The brain-compatible curriculum.

For All

Teaching

Assessment

Curriculum

Technology

Learning

How does integrated mathematics instruction affect teaching and learning?

Research and Ideas to Know About

The Learning Principle of the NCTM *Principles and Standards for School Mathematics (PSSM)* urges that classrooms be places where students regularly "engage in tasks and experiences designed to deepen and connect their knowledge." (p. 21) Teachers facilitate the development of these connections when they integrate content and instruction.

When mathematics is taught in rich and realistic contexts, rather than on a purely abstract basis, more students are able to build deep understanding. Conclusions from cognitive science indicate that knowledge taught in multiple contexts better supports permanent, functional learning of concepts. Students provided rich, demanding problems that build on, rather than simply repeat previous learning, grow in understanding. International studies indicate that teachers in successful classrooms orchestrate learning by providing problems where students apply prior learning to new problems. Students who learn mathematics through complex problems and projects outperform other students whose learning is more compartmentalized and abstract. Particularly, they apply relevant previous learning to new problem situations, incorporating common sense and confidence with their mathematics skills in order to reach a solution.

Business and industry require workers who can think and solve problems and who have integrated their knowledge. School experiences need to help build this integration. Real problems do not come neatly divided into mathematics strands. Often they require collecting real data (statistics and measurements), representing it visually (e.g., with coordinate geometry), then determining an equation that closely approximates the shape of the data (algebra) in order to predict future values for the situation (probability).

Through classrooms that provide rich problem-solving situations as a way to learn mathematics, students develop a flexible understanding of the discipline and learn to integrate content and process strands of mathematics. They learn when, how, and why to use their knowledge to solve unfamiliar problems.

> When mathematics is taught in rich and realistic contexts... more students are able to build deep understanding.

Implications to Think About

Integrating the various branches of mathematics not only makes sense, it also saves time. Time is always a factor in student learning, and for students to build understanding, topics must be addressed with sufficient depth. The key may be to teach related topics together.

A variety of mathematics programs supporting integrated instruction are available for all grade levels. Each uses challenging contextual problems to develop understanding of important mathematics. Programs from the past often have not helped students make connections within mathematics or with other subjects. At the elementary level, though text materials usually contain chapters on various mathematics strands, each is isolated. Meanwhile, the conclusions of cognitive science indicate the importance of making connections in order to transfer learning.

Teachers new to integrated mathematics might learn by using problems from these programs and observing their students. They might also examine the growing number of achievement studies of students in integrated programs.

Here are some considerations regarding an integrated approach to mathematics instruction

- Engagement does not guarantee learning. Students can be interested without learning new mathematics.
- Allowing students to struggle enhances learning. Students need to struggle with a problem they do not know how to solve, but to which they can apply known mathematics.
- True integration is not obvious by casual observation. An assortment of topics in a program doesn't necessarily indicate that the content is integrated. A teacher must see, through teaching, how ideas connect and are built upon.

One of the most important roles for a mathematics teacher is to select rich, integrated mathematical tasks and problems, ones that are accessible for all students, yet challenging enough to help them grow in mathematical understanding.

Resources for Learning More

Boaler, J. (1997). Experiencing school mathematics.

Bransford, J. D., Brown, A. L., & Cocking, R. R. (Eds.) (2000). How people learn.

Dogan-Dunlap, H. (2004). Changing students' perception of mathematics through an integrated, collaborative, field-based approach to teaching and learning mathematics.

Froelich, G. (1991). Connecting mathematics.

Hiebert, J., Carpenter, T. P., Fennema, E., Fuson, K. C., et al. (1997) Making sense.

Hiebert, J. (1999) Relationship between research and the NCTM Standards.

National Council of Teachers of Mathematics. (2000). Principles and standards for school mathematics.

Stigler, J. W., & Hiebert, J. (1999). The teaching gap.

Trammel, B. (2001). Integrated mathematics? Yes, but teachers need support!

For All

Teaching

Assessment

Curriculum

Technology

Learning

How does classroom curriculum connect to the outside world?

"We should all learn mathematics because it is useful, beautiful, and fun...Teachers of mathematics are obliged, I believe, to do everything in their power to help their students experience the joy of mathematics."

-Willoughby, S. S., 2000, p. 10-11.

Research and Ideas to Know About

Children learn both inside and outside the classroom. Mathematics teachers must connect these two realms of knowledge and use the connections to augment understanding of both worlds. Real life is a rich source of mathematics problems. Learning is highly interactive as students explore problems, formulate ideas, and check those ideas with peers and with their teacher through discussion and collaboration. Students build new concepts as they recognize the connections between previous learning, intuition, formalized structures, mathematical strands, and other disciplines. Students create mathematical tools and aids—symbols, schemas, and visual models—during the learning process to move from concrete reality to more abstract higher level thinking skills.

School mathematics has shifted away from a fixed body of knowledge calling for the mechanistic manipulation of numbers, symbols, and geometric proofs. Today, learning mathematics involves discovering why techniques work, investigating multiple approaches to problem solving, and justifying solutions.

Questions teachers should ask when selecting tasks that help connect the classroom to the outside world include these

- Do the tasks build on prior knowledge? Proceed from informal ideas to more formal understanding? Increase in complexity? Connect to other mathematics domain strands and to other disciplines?

- Do the tasks lead to model construction, evaluation, and revision?

- Do the tasks lead to inquiry and justification? Is the student asked to make conjectures? Formulate a solution plan? Solve? Conclude and justify that conclusion?

- Do the tasks lead students to self-question? Question others? Research? Evaluate and reevaluate?

- Are the tasks relevant to students? Is there intrinsic motivation in the tasks? Do they foster personal ownership? Do they allow for unique approaches based on an individual's own knowledge? Are the tasks challenging enough to be engaging, but not so challenging that they produce too much cognitive conflict?

Implications to Think About

Mathematics teachers need to know mathematics content, mathematics pedagogy, and how their students understand mathematical concepts. To design an appropriate curriculum, teachers need to know their students and their families, as well as their activities and interests.

Teachers need to understand and use the "Big Ideas" of mathematics; that is, ideas that are central to the learning of mathematics—ones that link mathematical understandings into a coherent whole (Charles, 2005). Teachers should consistently connect new ideas to these Big Ideas and reinforce them throughout their instruction.

Teachers must be familiar with their students' mathematical strengths, misconceptions, favorite problem-solving approaches, and readiness to use mathematical tools. Since engaging mathematics capitalizes on realistic settings, the context of investigations is important. For instance, if students work problems that ask them to cut pizzas for fair sharing, the rational number concepts associated with such divisions will be more memorable. When problems connect to the real world, learning becomes memorable.

Selecting problems for students to solve is one of the most important things a mathematics teacher does. Criteria for selecting problems include these

- Engage students' thinking.
- Focus on the development of conceptual understanding.
- Build skill proficiency through contextual application.
- Help students make connections and develop frameworks for ideas.
- Ask students to formulate questions and reason mathematically.
- Promote communication about mathematics.
- Acknowledge diverse backgrounds and develop all students' dispositions to do mathematics.
- Promote the variety of occupations that identify mathematics as being important.

Textbook companies continue to develop materials that support standards-based mathematics teaching through curriculum design that connects students to the world outside the classroom.

Resources for Learning More

Charles, R. I. (2005). Big ideas and understandings as the foundation for elementary and middle school mathematics.

Keleher, L. A. (2006). Building a career mathematics file.

Ma, L. (1999). Knowing and teaching elementary mathematics.

National Council of Teachers of Mathematics. (1989). Curriculum and evaluation standards for school mathematics.

National Council of Teachers of Mathematics. (2007). Mathematics teaching today.

National Council of Teachers of Mathematics. (2000). Principles and standards for school mathematics.

Romberg, T., & Kaput, J. (1999). Mathematics worth teaching, mathematics worth understanding.

Willoughby, S. S. (2000). Perspectives on mathematics education.

For All

Teaching

Assessment

Curriculum

Technology

Learning

Instructional Technology in Mathematics

Instructional technology refers to the tools used to promote classroom learning. In mathematics teaching, instructional technology is often used in problem solving, thereby making the learning experience more learner-centered. Specific technologies include various types of calculators, handheld data-collection devices, computers, associated software, and the Internet.

Instructional technologies such as those found in *Using Technology with Classroom Instruction that Works* (Pitler, et al., 2007) add relevancy and increase student engagement. Further benefits for mathematics instruction include increased accuracy and speed in data collection and graphing; real-time visualization; interactive modeling of ambiguous mathematical processes; ability to collect, compute, and analyze large volumes of data; collaboration for data collection and interpretation; and greater opportunity to vary the presentation of results. Technology can make mathematics more meaningful and standards more attainable for all students. The Technology Principle from the National Council of Teachers of Mathematics (NCTM) *Principles and Standards for School Mathematics (PSSM)* states "technology should be used widely and responsibly, with the goal of enriching students' learning of mathematics." (pg. 25)

How can using instructional technology affect mathematics reasoning and problem solving?

Technology allows us to teach traditional topics in new ways as well as teach new topics that are only accessible with technology.

Research and Ideas to Know About

Schooling should mirror the many ways mathematicians have taken advantage of the technologies available to them. Whether it be constructing a bisector of an angle with straightedge and compass or designing a bridge using Computer Assisted Design, technology tools are an important part of a mathematics program. Technology allows us to teach traditional topics in new ways as well as teach new topics that are only accessible with technology. Computer-Assisted Instruction continues to grow, and programs now include complex problem-solving software that permits students to address problems in individual ways. Students can try things out, see the consequences, and then refine their thinking, thereby constructing their own knowledge. Many of these programs are in a gaming format that incorporates continual feedback mechanisms and differentiation to readily engage students. Although current research is insufficient to state conclusively the impact of instructional software, the final report of the National Mathematics Advisory Panel indicates that when implemented appropriately, high-quality instructional software can exert positive effects on student achievement. The panel recommends continued research on which critical features of software contribute to learning.

Online or handheld calculators permit students to check their work or attack a problem differently. Certain fraction calculators permit students to choose a common factor in order to simplify improper fractions. Graphing calculators can reduce the need to manipulate algebraic expressions or equations. They can help students see the connection between algebra and analytic geometry. Studies show that students who learn in a technological environment with a related algebra curriculum perform better on standard algebra manipulations as well as modeling and problem solving.

Sensor probes, when used with computers or graphing calculators, can obtain real-time data. The Internet permits students to obtain real data from all over the world. Employing such sets of data makes mathematics come alive. Specifically, technology increases the engagement level of urban youth in mathematics. Students using such technologies are likely to show greater persistence in solving problems and are more apt to take risks. Hence, they are more likely to become productive citizens in the global, digital information-based society of the 21st century.

Implications to Think About

Two concerns must be addressed when using technology: how and why to use it. Students still need to know the basic facts and most of the algorithms used in a traditional mathematics program. Using technology to better teach these fundamental tenets does not imply their irrelevance. Technology should be integrated into mathematics instruction as a modern tool of instruction. The NCTM Technology Principle emphasizes that tools allow students to focus on decision making, reflection, reasoning, collaboration, and problem solving without being replacements for basic understanding.

Additionally, teachers must assure equity within their school. These technologies are not just for the remedial or the advanced student; they allow teachers to provide differentiated instruction and meet the needs of all students. When used properly, technology motivates students to become more interested in mathematics. A student can conjecture and explore possible solutions. Some technology tools permit students with limited physical abilities to fully participate.

Instructional technology is constantly evolving. Teachers should be flexible, creative, and knowledgeable of its use and influence on student achievement. Technological devices permit students to work independently or in teams, with the teacher as a facilitator or fellow problem solver. Current instructional technology innovations, such as competency computer-based programs, allow teachers to present concepts in new and exciting ways.

Teachers must invest time and effort in learning these new approaches on their own or through professional development. When teachers understand the many potential uses of instructional technology, they can assess its utility in their mathematics program.

Resources for Learning More

Mistretta, R. (2005). Integrating technology into the mathematics classroom.

Moses, R. P., & Cobb, Jr., C. E. (2001). Radical equations.

National Council of Teachers of Mathematics. (2008). The role of technology in the learning and teaching of mathematics.

National Council of Teachers of Mathematics. (2000). Principles and standards for school mathematics.

National Mathematics Advisory Panel. (2008). Foundations for success: Final report.

National Research Council (2003). Engaging schools.

Pitler, H., Hubbell, E. R., Kuhn, M., & Malenoski, K. (2007). Using technology with classroom instruction that works.

The algebra project. [Web site] http://www.algebra.org/

Tomlinson, C. A. (2003). Fulfilling the promise of the differentiated classroom.

Ysseldyke, J., & Bolt, D. (2007). Effect of technology-enhanced continuous progress monitoring on math achievement.

For All

Teaching

Assessment

Curriculum

Technology

Learning

What effect do calculators have on student learning?

As with any instructional tool, the learning goal of the lesson should determine whether use of a calculator is appropriate.

Research and Ideas to Know About

After students master the underlying concepts behind calculations, they can use calculators to expand their abilities. Calculators play a larger role than simply replacing paper-and-pencil computation. By efficiently processing lower level calculations, calculators allow students to analyze, synthesize and create larger mathematical concepts. Potential uses include developing number sense, exploring mathematical concepts such as geometry, representing and graphing data, and solving complex problems.

Although the use of calculators in the mathematics classroom has been only minimally explored by researchers, some findings suggest that when calculators are used in a variety of ways, students perform as well as, or better than, those who use paper-and-pencil methods. Internationally, as students' in-class calculator use has increased, so has their level of performance on mathematics assessments. However, the final report of the National Mathematics Advisory Panel cautions that overuse of calculators may impede the development of automaticity and fluency in computation. The report states that this was a particular concern from the survey of Algebra I teachers. As with any instructional tool, the learning goal of the lesson should determine whether use of a calculator is appropriate. If the learning goal is fluency with whole number computation, then use of a calculator may not be appropriate. However, if the learning goal involves more complex problem solving, then the calculator may be a valuable tool to promote mathematical reasoning.

Students using calculators

- Have higher math achievement than non-calculator users even when they can choose any tool desired.
- Do better on mental computation than non-calculator users.
- Experience more varied concepts and computations.
- Have improved attitudes toward mathematics.
- Do not become overly reliant on calculators.

Computing technologies enhance both the teaching and learning of mathematics when they are used to enable student exploration and to promote generalizations. Furthermore, studies indicate that gender differences disappear on student performance when students use graphing calculators.

Implications to Think About

Teachers can use the advantages of calculators, such as speed, to enhance student learning. Extra time allows students to try different approaches to problem solving. Students can work multiple problems or solve more difficult ones using a calculator in the same amount of time as the paper-and-pencil method. Calculators allow students to move at their own pace and concentrate on the mathematics of problem solving rather than on computations. Students who do not have full computational competencies can solve problems that are intellectually challenging.

The use of online or handheld graphing calculators can enhance inquiry learning by prompting more student discussions. The teacher can become the facilitator in the classroom while the students investigate the mathematical concepts, such as slope of a line or matrix multiplication.

Teachers can capitalize on the appropriate use of this technology to expand students' mathematical reasoning, not to replace it. Studies show that mathematical problem solving can be enhanced by calculator use because students

- Feel more confident in initiating problem solving.
- Do more exploration.
- Focus more on the problem to be solved and less on the algorithm for solving.
- Explain their strategies through deductive reasoning more consistently and interpret answers more readily.
- Are more successful if weak in basic facts.

Using calculators in carefully planned ways can result in increases in student problem-solving ability and improved affective outcomes without a loss of basic skills. Students need to learn the capabilities of the various technologies, including calculators. Knowing what each tool can do allows students to determine which tool to select for which purpose—and whether or not to use a tool at all. A skillful teacher knows how to help students develop these abilities in a balanced program focusing on mathematical thinking, fluency, and understanding.

Resources for Learning More

Cawelti, G. (Ed.). (2004). Handbook of research on improving student achievement.

Groves, S., & Stacey, K. (1998). Calculators in primary mathematics.

Hembree, R., & Dessart, D. (1986). Effects of hand held calculators in pre-college mathematics education.

Johnson, J. (2000). Teaching and learning mathematics.

Leinhardt, G., Zaslavsky, O., & Stein, M. K. (1990). Functions, graphs, and graphing: Tasks, learning, and teaching.

Moschkovich, J., & Schoenfeld, A. H. (1993). Aspects of understanding.

National Council of Teachers of Mathematics. (2005, May). Computation, calculators, and common sense.

National Mathematics Advisory Panel. (2008). Foundations for success.

For All

Teaching

Assessment

Curriculum

Technology

Learning

What effect does technology have on the mathematics classroom learning environment?

"If you use graphing calculators, you arouse their interest. Students do not open a math book and say, 'Let me show you what I know on this page,' but they will show you what they know about a single button on a graphing calculator."

-Moses, R. P., & Cobb, C. E., Jr., 2001, p.117.

Research and Ideas to Know About

Integrating technology into instruction tends to move classrooms toward an environment where students work cooperatively, make choices more often, and more actively take part in their learning. Instructional technology empowers students by improving their skills and concepts through multiple representations; enhanced visualization; increased construction of mathematics meaning; and individualized and customized diagnoses, remediation, and evaluation.

Instructional technology facilitates

- Visualization of mathematical ideas.
- Organization and analysis of data.
- Computational efficiency and accuracy.

Many instructional technologies are tools for problem solving. Calculators, spreadsheets, graphing programs, function probes, "mathematical supposers" for making and checking conjectures, and programs modeling complex phenomena provide cognitive scaffolds to promote complex thinking, design, and learning. Using technological tools, students can become more motivated to learn and encouraged to think critically, which leads to lasting knowledge.

Technology allows students more autonomy in practicing higher order thinking skills and frees them to analyze, synthesize, and evaluate. For example, increased access to primary resources and large data sets broadens students' learning contexts and provides more opportunity for them to design real-world investigations. Real-world problems can make learning mathematics more exciting for students. Instructional technology allows them to communicate with working mathematicians and gather data in various environments. In addition, students define problems that interest them and can receive instantaneous feedback on the accuracy of their ideas.

Instructional technology also broadens the learning community. When students collaborate, they share the process of constructing ideas, often reflecting on them in ways generally not seen in classrooms. Web 2.0 applications, such as video sharing, wikis, blogs, and podcasts, allow students to show projects to and collaborate with students from around the world. With technology, students can productively pursue their interests with fewer time constraints and intellectual barriers, thereby maximizing creativity, individuality, and desire to learn.

Implications to Think About

When students experience mathematics integrated with technology, the learning environment changes. The teacher, as a facilitator, moves throughout the classroom, assisting individual children or the group as a whole. The teacher's role is to help students internalize concepts that can be derived from symbols, graphs, or other technological representations of mathematics.

Instructional technology allows students to use a variety of design strategies such as problem solving, creative and critical thinking, visual imagery, and reasoning; hands-on abilities such as measuring, drawing and sketching, working with computers, and using tools; and quality control mechanisms, such as assessment and evaluative techniques. When students design their own learning environments, they can become skilled in the use and maintenance of technological products and systems, and they can assess the appropriateness of these tools and systems.

It is not the equipment in the classroom, but how the equipment is used that makes the difference in student understanding. For example, tools such as dynamic geometry software allow students to construct mathematical knowledge rather than memorize facts and formulas. The keys to success lie in finding the appropriate points for integrating technology into mathematics and making sure the resources are available often enough to support student understanding and reflection.

When teachers prepare to integrate technology, they should be guided by the following planning questions

1. What knowledge will students learn?
2. Which strategies will provide evidence that students have learned that knowledge?
3. Which strategies will help students acquire and integrate that knowledge?
4. Which strategies will help students practice, review, and apply the knowledge?

Once these questions have been answered, teachers are ready to select supporting technologies.

Resources for Learning More

Bransford, J. D., Brown, A. L., & Cocking, R. R. (Eds.). (2000). How people learn.

Burke, M. J., & Curcio, F. R. (Eds.). (2000). Learning mathematics for a new century.

Cuoco, A. A. (Ed.). (2001). The roles of representation in school mathematics.

Friedman, M. I., Harwell, D. H., & Schnepel, K. C. (2006) Effective instruction.

International Society for Technology in Education. (2007). National educational technology standards for students.

International Technology Education Association. (2000). Standards for technological literacy.

Moses, R. P., & Cobb, C. E., Jr. (2001). Radical equations.

Pitler, H., Hubbell, E. R., Kuhn, M., & Malenoski, K. (2007). Using technology with classroom instruction that works.

Van't Hooft, M. & Swan, K. (Eds.). (2006). Ubiquitous computing in education.

For All

Teaching

Assessment

Curriculum

Technology

Learning

How can students best use information and data from the Internet and Web 2.0 applications?

Using current real-world data provides mathematics teachers and students with an enriching resource that cannot be duplicated in a textbook.

Research and Ideas to Know About

The *PSSM* Technology Principle emphasizes that instructional technology tools allow students to focus on decision making, reflection, reasoning, and problem solving, and to enhance basic understanding. Many of these tools are freely available on the Internet. Students can use the Internet to access any learning resource at any time from any place. However, realizing that information on the Internet is only as good as its source, students should spend time learning how to evaluate and select reputable, usable information.

Using current real-world data provides mathematics teachers and students with an enriching resource that cannot be duplicated in a textbook. For instance, working on a physics, engineering, or computer science problem that is in the news sparks student interest and may relate to what is being studied in other classes. Real data answers the question, "What is this good for?" Population figures, acid rain amounts, or the latest medical breakthroughs are data that can be used in mathematics classroom activities.

Real-world data tends to be messier than data sets supplied in textbooks; no longer does the data set for a particular problem have to result in integral solutions. Computer software and sophisticated online calculators can give students access to methods for solving problems using real data. Technology permits them to ask and try to answer their own questions generated by the data.

There are many resources available on the Internet to help students embrace collaborative learning. Web 2.0, or the read/write Web, has opened up a whole new world for students to collaborate, share, and get feedback on their work. Math blogs are Web pages used by teachers to organize their classes and provide discussion forums for reflection, e-portfolios, student-student critiques, and project based learning. Wikis are collaboratively built "living Web pages" used by students for team projects and by teachers for math curriculum mapping. Podcasts allow students to listen to a class lesson as review or to make their own commentary on mathematics topics. Social bookmarking services let students and teachers share trusted e-resources; social media provides for sharing images and videos and allows teachers to collaborate with other professionals with common interests anywhere in the world.

Implications to Think About

Students live in the information age. They read and hear of happenings around the world that interest them. Teachers can take advantage of this interest by using data from the Internet to provide the context for mathematics lessons. Furthermore, they can leverage the power of Web 2.0 applications to manipulate this data in new and engaging ways.

Looking at population growth patterns in various states or countries, students can graph the data and make predictions about the size of future generations. Middle-level students might estimate the slopes of lines or curves and discuss interpretations, while high school students might use their technologies to find regression lines of best fit.

In addition to taking data from Web sites, students might communicate with others about data and related mathematical procedures. Presenting data and the conclusions reached from that data does not come easily, and students benefit from multiple opportunities to practice. Students can exchange data and share calculations, interpretations, and reports on a variety of topics, such as weather or voter preferences.

Students also can sharpen their research skills by using search engines and Web site evaluation tools. Teachers should carefully screen Internet sites before student use, evaluate the credibility of the sources, and determine the usefulness of the data. Some sites contain data sets that may be too extensive, complex, or in an inaccessible format for the intended instructional purpose. While evaluation of sources is initially a teacher responsibility, students also should learn how to recognize legitimate Web sites that report accurate data.

Before and during the use of Web 2.0 applications, students should be taught proper online etiquette and safety precautions, such as never post your contact information or full name and report any inappropriate contacts with strangers. Many online applications have safety and privacy features built into the programs. Teachers should familiarize themselves with these features and use them to keep the learning environment safe and honest without stifling student access and creativity.

Resources for Learning More

Beck, S. (2007). The good, the bad and the ugly.

Frand, J. L. (2000). The information-age mindset.

International Society for Technology Education. (2007). National education technology standards for students.

Kathy Schrock's guide for educators. [Web site] http://school.discoveryeducation.com/schoolguide

Land, S. M., & Greene, B. A. (2000). Project-based learning with the World Wide Web.

National Council of Teachers of Mathematics. (2000). Principles and standards for school mathematics.

Pitler, H., Hubbell, E. R., Kuhn, M., & Malenoski, K. (2007). Using technology with classroom instruction that works.

Roempler, K. S. (2002, July). Search smarter.

For All

Teaching

Assessment

Curriculum

Technology

Learning

How has technology changed the mathematics that is important for students to learn?

Research and Ideas to Know About

Most mathematics teachers understand that the use of classroom technology strongly affects how mathematics is taught. Its use also influences the content and order of the mathematics curriculum. Some topics become more important because effective use of technology requires their understanding. These include number sense, rounding, establishment of range and domain, and communication through spreadsheets. Others become less important because the use of calculator and computer technology replaces them. These include multi-digit computation, complicated factoring, and hand drawing complex graphs. Technology allows some new mathematics content to be added to the curriculum because it provides easy access. This includes several topics which relate to the world of work, including working with large matrices, continuous compounding of interest, and creation and interpretation of fractals and statistics.

Through instructional technologies, students and teachers are better able to

- Engage in meaningful and challenging mathematics tasks.
- Interact with mathematical ideas in innovative ways that allow active student participation.
- Build knowledge that reflects different models of instruction and different approaches to the learning of mathematics.

Online and handheld calculators, dynamic software, and computer simulations are a few technology tools that permit investigation of the relationships within and between mathematical topics. Students make connections among various mathematical ideas while exploring relationships efficiently by using such tools.

Achievement in higher order thinking skills is positively related to the use of technology. These technologies allow students to observe mathematically accurate patterns and to form conjectures. Students' problem-solving techniques and deductive reasoning skills grow stronger because they can seek answers to their own "what-if" questions.

Through technology, mathematics students have access to fields of mathematics previously reserved for experts.

Implications to Think About

The use of instructional technologies in the mathematics classroom not only increases the types of content that can be taught, it also may decrease the utility of some traditional content. Decisions about what is or is not obsolete mathematics content must be made thoughtfully, recognizing not just what technology can do, but analyzing carefully what students need to be able to do and how they need to be able to reason. The curriculum must still be about the mathematics, not about the technology. The most important instructional decision is how the technology fits with the purpose of the lesson.

The choice of problems posed in the mathematics classroom is critical to learning. Technology changes the pool of potential problems and the ways to present them. Mathematics teachers incorporating technology into the curriculum should

- Create a vision for the best use of technology in classrooms.
- Choose technologies that support established learning goals.
- Determine whether a selected technology interferes with the development of a needed skill or if it promotes the students' ability to think independently of the technology.
- Provide resources to help students gain power and fluency with technological tools.
- Adapt technology for individual student needs.

Technology offers teachers the opportunity to differentiate instruction and change their classrooms into dynamic learning environments. No longer do teachers have to "teach to the middle" as sophisticated software can adjust to each student's progress and keep them challenged yet engaged in their learning.

The No Child Left Behind Act specifically identifies technology as one way to enhance education. Administrators must ensure current use and practice for integrating technology in mathematics instruction by providing adequate and ongoing support through high-quality professional development.

Resources for Learning More

Brown, J., Collins, A., & Duguid, P. (1989). Situated cognition and the culture of learning.

Forum on Education Statistics. (2002). Technology in schools.

Groves, S., & Stacey, K. (1998). Calculators in primary mathematics.

Johnson, J. (2000). Teaching and learning mathematics.

Kleiman, G. M. (2004). What does the research say?

Lawrenz, F. Gravely, A., & Ooms, A. (2006, March). Perceived helpfulness and amount of use of technology in science and mathematics classes at different grade levels.

North Central Regional Educational Laboratory. (2005). Critical Issue: Using technology to improve student achievement.

Pitler, H., Hubbell, E. R., Kuhn, M., & Malenoski, K. (2007). Using technology with classroom instruction that works.

Schmidt, M.E. & Vandewater, w (2008, Spring). Media and attention, cognition, and school achievement.

For All

Teaching

Assessment

Curriculum

Technology

Learning

Learning Mathematics

What does it mean to learn mathematics? This question is addressed in the National Council of Teachers of Mathematics (NCTM) *Principles and Standards for School Mathematics (PSSM)*. Children are natural learners. They are inquisitive about patterns and shapes, recognizing and creating them from a young age. They count, measure, and share objects. For children, mathematics is learned by doing. Their school experience of mathematics learning should include problem solving and reasoning through grade 12, not simply lectures, books, and worksheets.

During the twentieth century, educators' understanding of the learning process progressed from behavioral observations through cognitive psychology into improved knowledge about neurophysiology. The 1990s were dubbed "the decade of the brain" because of the tremendous increase in understanding of how the brain works. Twenty-first century educators are improving their classroom practice through application of the newest understandings from neuroscience.

How can we communicate with the public about the importance of learning mathematics?

"In our technically oriented society, "innumeracy" has replaced illiteracy as our principal educational gap....[W]e live in an age of mathematics—the culture has been 'mathematized'."

- National Academy of Sciences, 1996.

Research and Ideas to Know About

The general public is more aware of mathematics education reform than in the past 30 years. Publications such as the National Commission of Education's *A Nation at Risk*, the standards-setting work of the National Council of Teachers of Mathematics, and media coverage of reports from TIMSS, the Program for International Student Assessment (PISA), and the final report of the National Mathematics Advisory Panel highlight the need for reform. Most people agree that mathematical literacy extends beyond knowledge of mathematics concepts and procedures into the ability to create mathematical models of situations, solve the problems represented by the models, and interpret the solutions in terms of societal implications.

The Glenn Commission Report, *Before It's Too Late*, cites four compelling reasons why students should become competent in mathematics and science: 1) the pace of change in the global economy and the American workplace, 2) the need for both mathematics and science in everyday decision-making, 3) national security interests, and 4) the intrinsic value of mathematics and science to our society. According to the National Science Board (2008), jobs related to STEM (science, technology, engineering, mathematics) are outpacing overall job growth by 3:1. The United States does not have enough domestic students to fill these jobs. With the anticipated growth in STEM jobs, promoting student interest in these fields is a national interest.

The value of learning mathematics today is best addressed in the context of mathematical literacy for all students. The NCTM standards, *Principles and Standards for School Mathematics (PSSM)* and other state, local, and national documents provide the specifications and framework for mathematical literacy. *PSSM* describes the vision, foundation, and goals for school mathematics. The vision is a future in which all students have access to rigorous, high-quality mathematics instruction, and all students value mathematics and engage actively in learning it. The Principles (equity, curriculum, teaching, learning, assessment, and technology) and the Standards (number and operations, algebra, geometry, measurement, data analysis and probability, problem solving, reasoning and proof, communications, connections, and representation) call for a common foundation of mathematics for all students.

Implications to Think About

Mathematical literacy is the goal for all students, not just for those preparing for college or for a career dependent on higher level mathematics. Mathematical literacy includes using mathematics-related knowledge on a personal and societal level, addressing issues by asking questions, using evidence to propose explanations or answers, and becoming informed citizens. Learning expectations must be high for all students. To promote the goal of mathematics literacy and the vision of quality mathematics education, the entire K–12 educational system must be aligned and focused on providing

- Important content in solid mathematics curricula.
- Competent and knowledgeable mathematics teachers who can integrate instruction and assessment.
- Education policies that support and enhance learning.
- Connections across disciplines.
- Mathematics classrooms with access to technology.
- Preparation for future careers.
- Tools and strategies to assist with making decisions on mathematics-based issues.

To offer high-quality, K–12 mathematics learning experiences for all students, there must be a consistent and coherent program taught by content-qualified teachers. Administrators can offer positive support by providing access to mathematics resources, ensuring that a competent mathematics teacher is in every classroom, and promoting ongoing opportunities for high-quality professional development. A principal message in the final report of the National Mathematics Advisory Panel cites the central role of knowledgeable mathematics teachers in mathematics education and encourages citizens and leadership to seek initiatives for recruiting, preparing, evaluating, and retaining effective teachers.

Outreach by mathematics educators to parents and the school community can help achieve a shared commitment to improve mathematics education. Because parent attitudes about mathematics predict student success, parents must help teachers guide students to an understanding of their critical need to learn mathematics.

Resources for Learning More

Campbell, P. (1992). Math, science, and your daughter.

Mirra, A. (2003). Administrator's guide: How to support and improve mathematics education in your school.

Mirra, A. (Ed.). (2004). A family's guide: Fostering your child's success in school mathematics.

National Academy of Sciences. (1996). Renewing U. S. mathematics.

National Commission on Excellence in Education. (1983). A nation at risk.

National Commission on Mathematics and Science Teaching for the 21st Century. (2000). Before it's too late.

National Council of Teachers of Mathematics. (2000). Principles and standards for school mathematics.

National Mathematics Advisory Panel. (2008). Foundations for success.

National Research Council. (1989). Everybody counts.

National Science Board. (2008). Science and engineering indicators 2008.

For All

Teaching

Assessment

Curriculum

Technology

Learning

What do we know about how students learn mathematics?

Students must have ample opportunities to learn, if they are to fully develop their mathematical proficiency.

Research and Ideas to Know About

Today's educators have a greater understanding of how students learn mathematics. The use of manipulatives, a focus on algebraic concepts throughout the mathematics program, problems set in meaningful contexts, and ample opportunities and time to learn all are important. Research indicates that manipulatives, in particular, can be effective in mathematics instruction. While primary teachers generally accept the importance of manipulatives, some studies of students' mathematics learning have created interest in the use of manipulatives across all grades. It is important, however, to keep the focus on mathematics, as students may learn only about the manipulative and miss the mathematics. Teachers must carefully choose activities and manipulatives to effectively support the introduction of abstract symbols.' A principal message of the final report of the National Mathematics Advisory Panel calls for use of instructional practices and strategies that are clearly known from rigorous research about how children learn.

Students may have difficulty making the transition from arithmetic to algebra, but research indicates that development of algebraic reasoning can be supported in elementary and middle school. Young students can learn algebra concepts, especially algebraic representation and the notion of variable and function, and basic concepts can be introduced as patterning and as a generalization of arithmetic. For example, students can look for and analyze patterns on a hundreds chart.

Students can learn best about mathematical topics through solving meaningful, contextual problems and through collaborative mathematical discussions. Students do benefit somewhat from seeing problems solved, but they receive the most benefit from solving problems themselves and having the opportunity to explain their thinking. High-quality mathematics talk about concepts, procedures, and problem solving helps students understand more deeply and clearly. Appropriate questioning techniques by both teacher and student enhance the development of student problem solving skills.

Students must have ample opportunities to learn if they are to fully develop their mathematical proficiency. Students need school time for regular, sustained engagement in the study of mathematics, including meaningful practice built on understanding. Student practice is enhanced with timely feedback on work.

Implications to Think About

School programs should provide rich activities involving number and operations that enable students to build on their informal learning or to learn without prior instruction. Students need to have experiences with concrete materials when learning concepts at any level, and instructional materials and classroom teaching should help students transition from the concrete to the abstract. In order for this to occur, teachers should select instructional materials that focus on the mathematics.

Students must have a thorough understanding of the base-ten and decimal place-value number representations and fluency with multi-digit numbers and decimal fractions. Students should experience learning activities from early elementary grades regarding algebraic concepts. In middle school, algebraic ideas should be developed in a more robust way and integrated with other concepts. For example, teachers could introduce the central ideas of calculus, such as rate of change, to students throughout elementary and middle school grades.

Teachers should spend significant class time developing mathematical ideas and methods. The mathematics classroom should provide rich opportunities for students to solve contextual problems in groups or individually. Classroom discourse should include discussion of mathematical connections, other solution methods, and mathematical justifications. Students should have opportunities to verbalize their thought processes and work collaboratively. Many students benefit from hearing what their peers are thinking.

Teacher questioning techniques should elicit students' thought processes and solution strategies and give students opportunities to clarify their understanding. Often, changing the form of a question from single-answer to one that allows students various ways to achieve an end result will increase student creativity and motivation. For example, beyond asking students to answer items like, "Simplify $4x + 3x$," students also could be asked questions like, "What are four ways to represent the function $y = 7x$?" The latter question assesses student understanding while stimulating more creative thought.

Resources for Learning More

Carpenter, T. P., Levi, L., & Farnsworth, V. (2000, Fall). Building a foundation for learning algebra in the elementary grades.

Chapin, S. H., O'Connor, C., & Anderson, N. C. Classroom. (2003). Discussions.

DeCorte, E., Greer, B., & Verschaffel, L. (1996). Mathematics teaching and learning.

Kilpatrick, J., Swafford, J., & Findell, B. (Eds.). (2001). Adding it up.

National Mathematics Advisory Panel. (2008). Foundations for success.

Schwartz, S. L. (2007). Teaching young children mathematics.

Sousa, D. (2007). How the brain learns mathematics. Assessment C

Williams, D. (2007, April). The what, why, and how of contextual teaching in a mathematics classroom.

For All

Teaching

Assessment

Curriculum

Technology

Learning

What does learning theory show teachers about how students learn mathematics?

A learning theory-based instructional approach offers students an opportunity to take control of their learning of mathematics through a more personal connection.

Research and Ideas to Know About

Knowledge changes throughout a person's development and is culturally and socially mediated. Students are not empty vessels to be filled with knowledge; rather, they build their own knowledge structures. The NCTM *Principles and Standards for School Mathematics* builds a case through its Learning Principle for going beyond rote memorization. "Students must learn mathematics with understanding, actively building new knowledge from experience and prior knowledge." (p. 20) Planning courses of action, weighing alternatives, applying prior knowledge to new ways of thinking or new ideas, and making sense of the world are instructional strategies supported by learning theory, as well as skills of informed citizenship.

The human brain searches for patterns in sensory input and memory. It analyzes complex information into component parts, and synthesizes simple facts into concepts. The brain initially pays primary attention to the emotional content of information but can be focused through metacognition. Because it is changed by every act of learning, whether intentional or peripheral, each brain is unique. To apply brain research on learning, mathematics teachers should link new instruction to students' prior knowledge by employing teaching strategies that draw on varied learning styles.

Teachers' use of learning theory encourages learning environments that are student-centered. When teachers align instruction about facts, procedures, and concepts, they help strengthen student learning about all three. When students connect new learning to previously learned material, subsequent learning becomes easier and students are more apt to experience a sense of mathematical power.

A learning theory-based instructional approach offers students an opportunity to take control of their learning of mathematics through a more personal connection, which gives greater meaning to the acquired knowledge or skill. A mathematics classroom organized to promote learning values and encourages student interaction and cooperation, provides access to learning materials from realistic contexts, and allows students to generate their own ways of learning.

Implications to Think About

Learning is not a passive activity. This belief provides a focus for educators to use learning theory in designing mathematics classrooms.

Teachers should correct any misconceptions about mathematics topics that students might have, yet changing long-held concepts in light of new information can be a complex and time-consuming process. Effective teaching requires not only sound knowledge of correct mathematics information, but also knowledge of common misconceptions and how to deal with them. Without the latter, students' attempts to combine new instruction with prior misconceptions can have unanticipated learning outcomes.

Effective mathematics teachers play a pivotal role in helping students search for deeper knowledge and skill. They probe for greater justification of student-generated ideas and deeper explanations of relationships and of how mathematics works using questions such as

- How does this operation work?
- What generalization can you make from this mathematical situation? Defend your ideas.
- What alternative strategy can you develop for this procedure?
- How can you justify your answer?
- What patterns or relationships apply to this problem? Describe the ones you found.

These types of questions emphasize student-to-student interactions and justification of their ideas, while valuing their knowledge and skill. The teacher, therefore, does not dominate the material or the conversation. Instead, the teacher's role is to help students shape their ideas while simultaneously honing their skills.

Students of teachers who plan instruction based on learning theory are more likely to take intellectual risks. They are willing to accept challenges to their misconceptions. Students who build new learning demonstrate their understanding rather than repeat what they are taught. Teachers who model building mathematical knowledge and who design learning environments that support it are honoring their students as emerging mathematicians.

Resources for Learning More

Bransford, J. D., Brown, A. L., & Cocking, R. R. (Eds.). (2000). How people learn.

Brooks, J. G., & Brooks, M. G. (1993). In search of understanding.

Caine, R. N., & Caine, G. (1994). Making connections.

Kilpatrick, J., Martin, W. G., & Schifter, D. (2003). A research companion to principles and standards for school mathematics.

National Council of Teachers of Mathematics. (2000). Principles and standards for school mathematics.

Phye, G. (Ed). (1997). Handbook of academic learning.

Ronis, D. (2006). Brain-compatible mathematics.

Schmidt, M.E. & Vandewater, E.A. (2008, Spring). Media and attention, cognition, and school achievement.

Sousa, D. A. (2005). How the brain learns.

Steffe, L. P., & Wiegel, H. G. (1996). On the nature of a model of mathematical learning.

For All

Teaching

Assessment

Curriculum

Technology

Learning

Learning Mathematics

What is the role of basic skills in mathematics instruction?

> "The automaticity in putting a skill to use frees up mental energy to focus on the more rigorous demands of a complicated problem."
>
> –Wu, H., 1999, p. 15.

Research and Ideas to Know About

An early definition of basic mathematical skills referred only to computation, arithmetic facts, and symbol manipulation. Today, it is clearly important that students solve problems, apply mathematics in everyday situations, use logical reasoning, and have an understanding of basic concepts of algebra, geometry, measurement, statistics or data analysis, and probability. All of these topics are incorporated in the new definition of basic mathematics skills.

Many of these topics that form the new definition of basic skills are discussed in other articles in this volume, so here we focus only on arithmetic. For example, command of addition, subtraction, multiplication, and division facts are essential in understanding computational processes. Students who commit basic facts to memory and become computationally fluent spend more time on the problem-solving process and thereby are more likely to become successful problem solvers. Automatic access to basic facts frees up a student's mental processes to allow directed focus on problem solving. The final report of the National Mathematics Advisory Panel cites fluency with whole numbers and fluency with fractions as critical components in student readiness for algebra coursework.

It is also important to note that there is abundant research evidence that proficient calculation skills and basic facts mastery need not precede conceptual understanding and problem solving. Students find well-chosen problems that are motivating and interesting to be an aid in learning and retaining mathematical ideas. Even basic facts can be learned relatively effortlessly through meaningful repetition in the context of solving problems or playing games. When students encounter a variety of contexts and tasks, they have more opportunity to develop and use thinking strategies that support and reinforce learning facts.

As mathematics teachers increasingly use the latest calculator and computer technologies, enhanced conceptions of basic skills in arithmetic and algebra are appearing. There is greater emphasis on number sense/symbol sense and strategies for mental computation and reasoned estimation. Reliance on paper-and-pencil routines for complex calculation has diminished as students have embraced the power of technology.

Implications to Think About

Students need to learn the most efficient strategies to master basic arithmetic facts. For example, 7 + 8 can be thought of as (7 + 7) + 1, and the answer to 7 x 8 can be determined from (5 x 8) + (2 x 8), or from (7 x 7) + 7. Such strategies rely on number sense and meaningful mathematical relationships. It is easier for students to learn new facts when they generate new knowledge rather than rely on memorization. Derived fact strategies improve recall and provide fall-back mechanisms for students. Facts and methods learned with understanding are connected, easier to remember and use, and can be reconstructed when forgotten. Learning with understanding is more powerful than simply memorizing because the act of organizing improves retention, promotes fluency, and facilitates learning related material.

Measurement skills that students learn in elementary school also are useful when they learn formal algebraic skills in high school. The product of the multiplication of two binomials (x + 2) and (x + 3) can be thought of as the area of a rectangle having sides with lengths (x + 2) and (x + 3). The result is one "big" square (x by x), five rectangles (1 by x), and 6 "little" squares, or $x^2 + 5x + 6$.

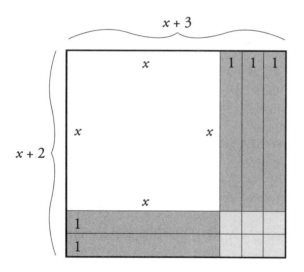

Procedural knowledge is best developed on a foundation of conceptual understanding. Practice toward mastery should not precede meaning. Drill does not guarantee immediate recall or contribute to growth in understanding. Practice is important, and once students understand a computation procedure, practice helps them become confident and competent in using it. But when students mimic a procedure without understanding, it is difficult for them to go back later and build understanding.

Resources for Learning More

Bass, H. (2003, Feb.) Computational fluency, algorithms, and mathematical proficiency.

Carpenter, T. P., Fenneman, E., Franke, M. L., et al. (1999). Children's mathematics.

Fuson, K. C. (1992). Research on learning and teaching addition and subtraction of whole numbers.

Hiebert, J., & Carpenter, T. P. (1992). Learning and teaching with understanding.

Johnson, J. (2000). Teaching and learning mathematics.

Kilpatrick, J., Swafford, J., & Findell, B. (Eds.). (2001). Adding it up.

National Council of Teachers of Mathematics. (2000). Principles and standards for school mathematics.

National Mathematics Advisory Panel. (2008). Foundations for success: Final report.

Wu, H. (1999, Fall). Basic skills versus conceptual understanding.

For All

Teaching

Assessment

Curriculum

Technology

Learning

What is the role of algorithms in mathematics instruction?

Understanding algorithms is central to developing computational fluency.

Research and Ideas to Know About

Algorithms and algorithmic study are important mathematical ideas that all students need to use and understand. An algorithm is a precise, step-by-step method or set of rules for solving a particular type of problem. Algorithmic study involves applying, developing, analyzing, and understanding the nature of algorithms. Although there are many types of algorithms in all fields of mathematics, we focus here on those associated with arithmetic operations.

Questions about the teaching of well established (standard or conventional) arithmetic algorithms are the subject of debate, especially between traditional and reform approaches. Research foci about algorithmic development and computational fluency include these: the value of standard, student-invented, and alternative algorithms; the value and place of drill in learning algorithms; and the place of algorithms in a technological world.

In order to become fluent in calculation, students must have efficient, accurate methods supported by number and operation sense, and they must know how algorithms work. Thoughtful use of standard algorithms advances fluency. However, rote learning of these traditional paper-and-pencil algorithms can interfere with the development of number sense. Further, early introduction and practice of algorithms may legitimize a single procedure and limit students' computational fluency so that they cannot choose methods that best fit the numbers or situation. The final report of the National Mathematics Advisory Panel states that curriculum must simultaneously develop conceptual understandings, computational fluency, and problem-solving skills.

Speed and efficiency in using arithmetic algorithms with large numbers is not as critical as it once was. There is little value in drilling to achieve such a goal. But many everyday mathematics tasks require facility with algorithms for computation. Technology has not made obsolete the need to understand and be able to perform some basic written algorithms.

Implications to Think About

Learning to use "standard" algorithms should be part of the mathematics curriculum. In addition to providing computational tools, algorithms can be important tools in their own right. They can be analyzed and compared, helping students understand the nature and properties of operations, place-value concepts for numbers, and characteristics of good algorithms.

Mathematics teachers need to understand the importance of alternative algorithms. Developing and discussing invented algorithms enhances students' number and operation sense. When students record, explain, and critique one another's strategies, they learn about efficiency, validity, and generalizability. A teacher can introduce various standard algorithms or note them as they arise naturally during discussions. Students will remember and implement algorithmic procedures better if they have time to make sense of them.

Appropriate practice is connected to mathematical thinking through reasoning, communicating, and problem solving. Appropriate practice reminds students that mathematics is well-structured (organized, filled with patterns, and predictable) and that the power of algorithms resides in their applicability as a tool for routine tasks and in the process of solving mathematics problems.

Learning a traditional algorithm means learning not only how to execute it with several examples, but also being able to explain its mathematical significance and prove that its various steps produce a correct answer. Understanding algorithms is central to developing computational fluency. Being able to compute fluently includes making smart choices about which tools to use and when. Students should have opportunities to choose among mental computation, paper-and-pencil algorithms, estimation, and calculator use. Ability to use algorithms enhances these choices.

Resources for Learning More

Bass, H. (2003, Feb.) Computational fluency, algorithms, and mathematical proficiency.

Carroll, W., & Porter, D. (1998). Alternative algorithms for whole-number operations.

Hiebert, J. (1999). Relationship between research and the NCTM standards.

Johnson, J. (2000). Teaching and learning mathematics.

Kamii, C., & Dominick, A. (1998). The harmful effects of algorithms in grades 1-4.

Kilpatrick, J., Swafford, J., & Findell, B. (Eds.). (2001). Adding it up.

National Council of Teachers of Mathematics. (2000). Principles and standards for school mathematics.

National Mathematics Advisory Panel. (2008). Foundations for success: Final report.

Steen, L. A. (1990). On the shoulders of giants.

For All

Teaching

Assessment

Curriculum

Technology

Learning

What factors contribute most strongly to students' success in learning mathematics?

One of the strongest predictors of students' success is the quality of their teacher.

Research and Ideas to Know About

One of the most important factors contributing to student success is active participation with mathematics Students who engage in mathematical modeling, problem solving, and reasoning apply the mathematics they are learning. Supporting practices include providing ample time to perform investigations, emphasizing discourse among students and between students and teachers, asking students to reflect on their work, allotting time to revise work, and acknowledging student diversity. The instructional practice of covering many discrete topics does not help students develop deep understanding and useful performance skills.

Teachers who set up active learning tasks that engage students in purposeful work spend substantial time moving about the classroom working with individuals and small groups. They make note of individual student accomplishments and needs, redirect students to new tasks as necessary, and listen as students reason their way through a problem. Students who experience a range of activity from short whole-group instruction to extended periods when they are engaged in problem solving are more likely to enjoy learning. A positive student-teacher relationship improves learning. In fact, research indicates that "social and intellectual support from peers and teachers is associated with higher mathematics performance for all students, and that such support is especially important for many African-American and Hispanic students." (final report of the National Mathematics Advisory Panel, p. 32)

One of the strongest predictors of students' success is the quality of their teacher. Teachers who are highly qualified with both mathematics content knowledge and pedagogical skills are more effective teachers. Teachers who continue their education while teaching tend to develop a deeper understanding of content applications, content knowledge, effective instructional strategies, theoretical bases for instructional decisions, and confidence in decision making. In general, teachers who continue learning throughout their careers are more likely to become conscientious, competent, professional teachers.

Implications to Think About

The teacher's instructional decision making contributes greatly to students' success in their mathematics classes. Those students who approach learning mathematics in realistic contexts, who work as mathematicians do, and who are held to the performance criteria of mathematicians, demonstrate the best understanding of mathematical concepts.

Class scheduling is of major importance to both administrators and teachers. Administrators need to examine teacher schedules to facilitate common planning time—a professional collegial time in which teachers design appropriate contextual problem-solving experiences for their students and cooperatively examine student work samples as a means of informing instruction. Teachers must provide classroom time for the in-depth study of major concepts in mathematics. Short, segmented class periods do not support the time necessary to explore topics in-depth or from multiple perspectives and often prevent students from achieving the flow and continuity of thinking that is so critical in making sense of mathematics.

Teachers help construct scaffolding for key ideas from students' prior knowledge, anticipate misconceptions, and design learning experiences that build on student thinking and reflect mathematics content aligned with the NCTM *Principles and Standards for School Mathematics*. Students need to be active listeners and be able to restate in their own words what others contribute. Students who are encouraged to try out new ideas, think aloud, and get specific feedback from others are more apt to internalize the mathematical concepts they are exploring. Teachers learn from watching and listening to their students and students learn by articulating what they know.

Successful mathematics students have teachers who stay current in mathematics as well as mathematics education. Effective mathematics teachers

- Read and apply relevant research in mathematics pedagogy and education.
- Keep abreast of changes in mathematics content.
- Are active members of their professional mathematics education organization.

Resources for Learning More

Barber, M. & Mourshed, M. (2007). How the world's best performing education systems come out on top.

Bransford, J. D., Brown, A. L., & Cocking, R. R. (Eds.). (2000). How people learn.

Darling-Hammond, L. (1997). The right to learn.

Hill, H. C., Rowan, B., & Loewenberg Ball, D. (2005). Effects of teachers' mathematical knowledge for teaching on student achievement.

Kilpatrick, W., Martin, G., & Schifter, D. (Eds.). (2003). A research companion to principles and standards for school mathematics.

Meier, D. (1995). The power of their ideas.

National Council of Teachers of Mathematics. (2000). Principles and standards for school mathematics.

National Mathematics Advisory Panel. (2008). Foundations for success.

Richard-Amato, P. A. Snow, M. A. (2005) Academic success for English language learners.

Stigler, J. W., & Hiebert, J. (1999). The teaching gap.

Tomlinson, C. A. (2003). Fulfilling the promise of the differentiated classroom.

For All

Teaching

Assessment

Curriculum

Technology

Learning

Learning Mathematics

How do students' attitudes affect their performance and future opportunities?

Students who enjoy mathematics tend to perform well in their mathematics course work.

Research and Ideas to Know About

Students' attitudes toward mathematics have a great effect on their achievement. Attitudes are stable dispositions, affective responses, or beliefs individuals have that develop largely through experience. Students who enjoy mathematics tend to perform well in their mathematics course work and are more likely to enroll in advanced courses. Conversely, those students who dislike mathematics tend not to do well in these classes, and/or do not attempt the more advanced mathematics classes in secondary school.

Negative attitudes about mathematics are learned, not inherited. Students enter school with a considerable amount of enthusiasm and curiosity that produces mathematical questions: What is the distance between my home and school? How likely am I to win this game? Do I have enough paint to finish this project? Students have positive emotions when they make mathematical conjectures, solve problems, and see connections between important ideas. Of course, students can also experience frustration when not making progress toward solving a problem. Teachers should provide appropriately challenging problems so students can learn and establish the norm of perseverance for successful problem solving.

Too often, mathematics instruction serves to alienate students rather than reveal to them its usefulness. A student with a productive attitude finds sense in mathematics, perceives it as useful and worthwhile, believes that steady effort in learning mathematics pays off, and views him or herself as an effective learner and doer of mathematics. Research suggests that students of color and females often learn early to doubt their mathematical abilities, and as a consequence, they are more likely to attribute failure to lack of ability. Generally, U. S. students are more likely to attribute success in mathematics problem solving to ability rather than effort. East Asian children, on the other hand, are more likely to perceive success as a function of effort, not ability. It is important for teachers to model perseverance, convey that mistakes and misconceptions are inevitable, and provide opportunities for learning. In addition, both students and teachers must believe that all students are able to learn mathematics.

Implications to Think About

The practices, culture, and norms of classrooms strongly influence student attitudes, particularly during elementary school years, when students' attitudes toward school and academics are forming. Findings suggest that among high poverty students, an emphasis on conformity, competition, and mathematics as rules decreases motivation and achievement when compared to a more exploratory curriculum. Students are less likely to think flexibly and critically when their schools emphasize order, obedience, an acceptance of school and mathematical rules, and a dependence upon the structures provided by these rules. While an organized learning environment is important, promoting students' comfortable exploration of mathematics through challenging open-ended problems should replace classroom norms that elevate procedures, rules, competition, and speed. However, while fostering students' positive attitudes toward mathematics, teachers need to be careful not to simplify a challenging curriculum or alleviate all of students' frustrations during problem solving.

Successful teachers communicate explicit expectations that students will adequately justify their answers, persist at problem solving when faced with frustration, and solve problems independently. Students of these teachers show satisfaction and enthusiasm for problem solving and demonstrate an autonomous view of themselves as learners. Effective mathematics teachers establish good relationships with students by being friendly rather than formal, sharing personal anecdotes that illustrate their own problem solving strengths and weaknesses, and establishing systems that hold students accountable for their performance. Most of these teachers focus on aspects of student performance other than obtaining correct answers. These teachers also tend to use cooperative groups to promote independence and to reduce students' frustration.

Fostering these desirable classroom norms with low-achieving students is equally critical. Teachers must provide all students with learning opportunities that allow them to make sense of mathematics.

Resources for Learning More

Boaler, J. (1997). Experiencing school mathematics.

Halpern, D., Aronson, J., Reimer, N., et al. (2007). Encouraging girls in math and science.

Henningsen, M., & Stein, M. (1997). Mathematical tasks and student cognition.

Kilpatrick, J., Swafford, J., & Findell, B. (Eds.). (2001). Adding it up.

Lester, F. K. (Ed.). (2007). Second handbook of research on mathematics teaching and learning.

Morge, S. P. (2007, August). Eliciting students' beliefs about who is good at mathematics.

Schackow, J. B., & Thompson, D. R. (2005, September). High school students' attitudes toward mathematics.

Stigler, J. W., & Hiebert, J. (2004). Improving mathematics teaching.

The algebra project. [Web site] http://www.algebra.org/

For All

Teaching

Assessment

Curriculum

Technology

Learning

How can teachers help students reflect on and communicate their own learning?

Metacognitive strategies, portfolios, and structured classroom writing assignments support students' personal construction of mathematics understanding.

Research and Ideas to Know About

Metacognition, sometimes referred to as thinking about thinking, is an excellent way to assist students to reflect on and to communicate their learning.

The use of metacognitive strategies, portfolios, and structured classroom writing assignments supports students' personal construction of mathematics understanding. Learning increases after explicit instruction in metacognitive strategies. Metacognitive strategies to manage thinking include

- Connecting newly learned information with information that is already known.
- Carefully choosing appropriate thinking strategies for a specific use.
- Planning, monitoring, and judging the effectiveness of thinking processes.

Creating and maintaining portfolios of personal work is one strategy that encourages reflection. The process of selecting and organizing the contents of a portfolio builds self-awareness. The use of classroom portfolios gives students more control over their own learning. It also supports the role of the teacher as a facilitator of learning.

Writing is another way for students to discover, organize, summarize, and communicate knowledge. Writing makes thinking processes concrete and increases retention of concepts. The act of writing gives students access to their thinking processes, enabling them to construct new understandings that are meaningful and applicable.

When students interact around the mathematics they are learning, they are better able to make connections among concepts and topics and to reorganize their knowledge. When students talk about the strategies, teachers can help them build on their informal knowledge. By facilitating classroom interactions, encouraging students to propose mathematical ideas, helping them learn to evaluate their own thinking and that of others, and developing their reasoning skills, teachers can enhance mathematics learning.

Implications to Think About

Students develop metacognitive strategies through frequent challenging problem solving. Metacognitive activities in mathematics classes can ask students to

- Identify what is known and not known (e.g., K-W-L – what I know/want to know/learned).
- Talk about thinking (first through teacher modeling, then in group discussion, culminating in paired problem solving).
- Maintain a thinking journal or learning log (e.g., a process diary).
- Take increased responsibility for planning activities.
- Practice targeted self-regulation skills following direct instruction (e.g., estimating time requirements, organizing materials, and scheduling).
- Debrief thinking processes during class closure (e.g., review thinking processes, identify and classify strategies used, evaluate successes, and seek alternatives).
- Participate in guided self-evaluation.

Writing tasks must be authentic; that is, the text must address a real audience, sometimes oneself. Students can use their journals to reflect on knowledge, feelings, and beliefs. Journals can open a dialogue between learner and teacher that leads to more individualized instruction and support. Throughout the year, topics for journal writing should start with affective, open-ended prompts (Describe a time when you felt successful in solving a mathematical problem. Why did you feel that way?), proceed to review of familiar mathematics concepts (How did you determine the line of symmetry?), and move toward discussion of more advanced mathematics concepts that extend and reinforce new understanding.

Other useful writing assignments include analytic essays, which develop links between concepts, and concept maps or hierarchical outlines, which can facilitate meaningful cooperative learning, identify misconceptions, evaluate understanding, and demonstrate construction of mathematical knowledge.

Resources for Learning More

Blakey, E., & Spence, S. (1990). Developing metacognition.

Bransford, J. D., Brown, A. L., & Cocking, R. R. (Eds.). (2000). How people learn.

Foster, G., Sawicki, E., Schaeffer, H., et al. (2002). I think, therefore I learn!

Goldberg, P. D., & Bush, W. S. (2003, September). Using metacognitive skills to improve 3rd graders' math problem solving.

Lester, F. K. (Ed.). (2007). Second handbook of research on mathematics teaching and learning.

National Council of Teachers of Mathematics. (2007). Mathematics teaching today.

National Council of Teachers of Mathematics. (2000). Principles and standards for school mathematics.

Pugalee, D. K. (2004, March). A comparison of verbal and written descriptions of students' problem solving processes.

Urquhart, V. A. & McIver, M. C. (2005). Teaching writing in the content areas.

Wisconsin Department of Public Instruction. (2007). Mathematics: Adolescent learning toolkit.

Wolfe, P. (2001). Brain matters: Translating research into classroom practice.

What role does active hands-on learning play in mathematics instruction?

When students can touch and move objects to make visual representations of mathematical concepts, different learning modalities are addressed.

Research and Ideas to Know About

Mathematical learning in young children is strongly linked to sense perception and concrete experience. Children move toward an understanding of symbols, and eventually abstract concepts, only after they have experienced ideas on a concrete level.

Mathematics achievement is increased through the long-term use of concrete instructional materials and active lessons at various grade levels. The more avenues there are to receive data through the senses, the more connections the brain can make, and the better a learner can understand a new idea. This holds not only for primary age learners, but through adulthood. All students need to learn mathematics by actively doing mathematics. This includes such activities as physically measuring objects, collecting and representing data, and handling geometric solids from the earliest ages. Other active learning experiences are representing numbers with locking cubes to put together and take apart groups of tens, sorting objects or cards containing pictures of shapes or mathematical objects, or using tiles to represent algebraic quantities. The National Library of Virtual Manipulatives offers free access to an interactive Web-based tool for further student engagement. Students also enjoy "acting out" problems or equations.

Students do not discover or understand mathematical concepts solely by manipulating concrete materials. Teachers must intervene frequently to help students focus on underlying mathematical ideas and to build bridges from the students' active work to their corresponding work with mathematical symbols or actions. It is important that students frequently reflect on their actions in relation to the mathematical concepts the teacher is promoting and the constraints of the task as they conceive it.

Despite the known benefits of hands-on learning, many mathematics teachers do not take full advantage of this strategy's effectiveness for learning. While most mathematics teachers have access to a variety of manipulatives such as Play-Doh, algebra and geometric tiles, and interactive, virtual manipulatives, they incorporate them into their lessons with varying frequency, if at all.

Implications to Think About

The kinds of experiences teachers provide play a major role in the extent and quality of a student's learning. Students' understanding will increase if they are actively engaged in tasks and experiences designed to deepen and connect their knowledge of mathematical concepts. Individual students learn in different ways. Through the use of manipulatives, various senses are brought into play. When students can touch and move objects to make visual representation of mathematical concepts, different learning modalities are addressed.

There is no single best method for mathematics instruction. However, we do know that any mathematics topic should involve multiple instructional techniques, allowing all students to develop a mathematical understanding through at least one method. For example, by presenting an activity with three components (manipulatives, technology, and formalizing), we not only give students with varied learning styles different ways to see a problem, we also give them extra time to process the concept.

Using manipulatives in combination with other hands-on instructional methods can enrich and deepen students' understanding. Appropriate use of concrete materials should be one component of a comprehensive mathematics education program.

Resources for Learning More

Compass Learning. Professional development [Web site] http://www.compasslearning.com/services/Development.aspx

Freer Weiss, D. M. (2006, January). Keeping it real.

Johnson, J. (2000). Teaching and learning mathematics.

Moyer, P. S., Bolyard, J. J., & Spikell, M. A. (2002, February). What are virtual manipulatives?

National Council of Teachers of Mathematics. (2000). Principles and standards for school mathematics.

National Library of Virtual Manipulatives [Web site] http://nlvm.usu.edu

Oliva, M. (2005). NCLB implementation center, building capacity through high-quality teachers.

Schackow, J. B. (2006). Using virtual manipulatives to model computation with fractions.

Sowell, E. J. (1989). Effects of manipulative materials in mathematics instruction.

Suh, J., & Moyer, P. S. (2007, April). Developing students' representational fluency using virtual and physical algebra balances.

For All

Teaching

Assessment

Curriculum

Technology

Learning

How does using contextual or applied activities improve student learning in mathematics?

Classroom activities with application to real world situations are the lessons students seem to learn from and appreciate the most.

Research and Ideas to Know About

Teachers have long thought that classroom activities with application to real-world situations are the lessons their students learn from and appreciate the most. Students have more meaningful learning experiences when mathematical concepts have a personal connection to their own lives, beyond a textbook or resource narrative. Today's students, who often are immersed in multimedia environments, are acclimated to multitasking and want to be participants in their learning experiences.

Brain research sheds light on why this is the case

- The more senses used in instruction, the better learners remember, retrieve, and connect information.
- Physical experiences or meaningful contexts provide learners with strong building blocks for knowledge.
- Acquiring new knowledge is enhanced when it is connected to what learners already know.
- Learning is most effective when people engage in "deliberate practice" that includes active monitoring of one's learning.

Information about memory creation and storage, learning, and complex connections helps explain why students learn through hands-on contextual activities. At the elementary level, many teachers use manipulative materials to provide contextual settings. The adage, "I hear and I forget; I see and I remember; I do and I understand," has been the hallmark in elementary education for many years and is supported by brain research.

Older students need similar experiences that involve physical materials or at least real-life contextual settings. Such activities encourage students to be responsible for their learning, to think critically, and to develop as future employees.

By incorporating realistic, integrated, or interdisciplinary activities that build on established knowledge and skills and more than one sense (seeing, hearing, or touching), memory pathways become more easily accessed and cross-referenced for future use. As the learner ages, the ease of access of learning pathways is directly dependent on stimulation from prior learning. Concepts embedded this way are truly learned. Students learn best when doing.

Implications to Think About

Since hands-on contextual activities help learning, teachers should include them in their lessons. If manipulative materials help to illustrate a new concept, use them. Young children may gain a better feeling for place value by chip trading or exchanging ten blue markers for one red marker or vice versa. Older students may gain a better understanding of solving an algebraic equation by working with manipulatives to physically build a representation of the equation, then solve it through moving the pieces.

Since real-life applied activities help learning, teachers should include a contextual setting for many of their lessons. The setting can motivate learning the concept, or it can illustrate it. Students' learning may be enhanced if they use their prior knowledge to construct and refine a new concept. For example, students trying to determine which school candidate has the best chance of winning the class presidency can conduct a valid survey by calling upon their knowledge of random sampling and probabilities.

Sources of problem based learning curricula and authentic assessments are widely available. Real-time data also is available on the Internet. Teachers can develop lessons that are based on students' interests to naturally make the connections between foundational concepts and an application.

Teachers might experiment with interdisciplinary applications as action research projects in the classroom. The teacher can develop a hypothesis for successful impact, implement the lesson, collect the data from students' performance, and analyze the data to see if the lesson had the desired result.

Understanding the learning process can become a fascinating study for all teachers. As teachers discover the most effective strategies for better student achievement, they can adapt their lessons accordingly.

Resources for Learning More

Bransford, J. D., Brown, A. L., & Cocking, R. R. (Eds.). (2000). How people learn.

Lester, F. K. (Ed.) (2007). Second handbook of research on mathematics teaching and learning.

Sousa, D. A. (2007). How the brain learns mathematics.

Williams, D. (2007, April 2007). The what, why, and how of contextual teaching in a mathematics classroom.

For All

Teaching

Assessment

Curriculum

Technology

Learning

What can parents do to support student learning in mathematics?

Inclusion of parents requires a planned and well-coordinated effort, which takes time.

Research and Ideas to Know About

Much research exsits on the effectiveness of parent involvement in increasing student achievement. When a school or district implements a well-designed and planned parent involvement effort, all students benefit, regardless of race, ethnicity, or income. Such programs are among the most accurate predictors of student achievement and success.

The National PTA recognizes parents as the primary influence in students' lives and necessary partners in their education. Parent involvement means that the parents or guardians of a student participate actively in a child's education. It ranges from volunteering in a student's classroom to reading with their child before bedtime to assuming leadership roles on school committees.

Parent involvement is ineffective when treated as an afterthought. Inclusion of parents requires a planned and well-coordinated effort, which takes time and may not be a priority. There are many benefits to having a well-designed program: higher grades; better attendance; increased motivation; improved self-esteem; consistent completion of homework; higher graduation rates; decreased alcohol use, violence, and antisocial behavior; and greater support and ratings of teachers by parents and community.

Successful parent involvement programs contain components that represent best practices and are addressed in the National PTA's standards:
1) Communicating—meaningful and consistent communication between home and school, 2) Parenting—parent training focused on parenting skills and current education topics, 3) Student learning—active participation in student learning at home, 4) Volunteering—varied and meaningful volunteer opportunities, 5) School decision making and advocacy—full partnership in decisions affecting children and families, and 6) Collaborating with community—use of community resources to enhance student learning and school-family partnerships. These standards assist educators, parents, and the community in developing or improving parent involvement programs within the context of locally identified needs.

Implications to Think About

Parents and children can enjoy mathematics together. With the proper resources and information, parents, families, and the community can become a teacher's greatest asset and support system.

Schools should begin communicating with parents early in the school year. Although most schools have open houses, a school could give parents an orientation to all of the opportunities available throughout the school year, including a brief introduction to standards, how parents can contact school staff and administration if they have concerns, and how different subjects are taught.

EQUALS and Family Math have excellent programs to show parents how to encourage mathematics learning and problem solving. The U. S. Department of Education and the National Science Foundation publish free parent resources that schools can send home with children. When schools use a non-traditional mathematics program, they can involve parents in doing the activities their student is learning, thus illustrating the mathematics content and processes. After this experience, most parents become advocates and spread their enthusiasm to others.

A child is more likely to complete homework when parents find the assignment relevant to their child's education, and when they have assistive guidelines. Many mathematics curricula and programs offer take-home activities and ideas for two-way contact with parents. A teacher can further support student learning by following up with parents about a certain activity.

Volunteering has traditionally meant direct participation on-site, including doing presentations or participating in Career Day. Volunteering could include activities done at home, such as calling Career Day panelists or creating presentation visuals. When alternatives are provided, more parents can participate.

Parents can be vital to decision making and advocacy work for schools, and they can help write proposals for additional funding for school programs. Partnerships enrich educational experiences both in content and context. Schools and local informal education facilities (e.g., zoos, planetariums, museums) can co-develop curricula. Community members can be mentors for mathematics careers, and businesses can allow a few hours a year for employed parents to volunteer or attend school conferences.

Resources for Learning More

Burns, M. (2007). About teaching mathematics.

Equals and family math. [Web site] http://www.lhs.berkeley.edu/equals/

Fromboluti, C. S., & Rinck, N. (1999). Early childhood.

Kilpatrick, J., & Swafford, J. (Eds.). (2002). Helping children learn mathematics.

Maynard, S., & Howley, A. (June 1997). Parent and community involvement in rural schools.

Mirra, A. (Ed.). (2004). A family's guide: Fostering your child's success in school mathematics.

National Council of Teachers of Mathematics. (2001). Figure this!

National Parent Teacher Association. (2004). National standards for parent/family involvement programs.

Parker, R. (2006). Supporting school mathematics.

Remillard, J. T., & Jackson, K. (2006). Old math, new math.

For All

Teaching

Assessment

Curriculum

Technology

Learning

What are characteristics of effective homework in mathematics?

Teachers should provide students with authentic learning opportunities to experience at home.

Research and Ideas to Know About

Daily, children face the obligatory question from parents: "What did you learn in school today?" The following day, the teacher asks, "Do you have your homework assignment?" Perhaps a better question would be, "What did you learn at home last night?" The home should be a place to extend mathematics learning.

Mathematics is in every aspect of life. Student learning in mathematics should always focus on understanding the set of skills and knowledge needed to investigate the world. Homework must emphasize developing students' mathematics skills to solve problems, which will help them understand the world. These mathematics skills are described as "process skills" in the NCTM *Principles and Standards for School Mathematics* and "habits of mind" in *Benchmarks for Science Literacy*.

Homework assignments provide the opportunity for students to do long-term projects that require multiple levels of understanding. Students take ownership when they spend weeks following stock prices in the newspaper, paying close attention to favorites, predicting industry trends, or perhaps even participating in an investment club. Watching TV and timing commercial breaks one night may be interesting, but when students keep data over a few weeks—timing commercials in different types of programs, making charts, and drawing graphs—their learning will go beyond the curriculum.

Homework time is an opportunity for students to reflect on learning and synthesize their mathematics understandings. Well-designed homework (e.g., charting weather patterns) can bring parents and other adults into a student's community of mathematics learners. Assignments should include students discussing their learning with others. This can be done through student learning teams, parent involvement, or the teacher-led electronic discussion groups. Teachers should provide students with authentic learning opportunities to experience at home.

Implications to Think About

Teachers who value problem-solving skills provide time in class to develop students' ability to solve problems and assign homework that uses these skills in new settings. Mathematics homework should not be schoolwork done at home; rather, work done in class should match homework. The home provides a unique opportunity for students to gain mathematics understanding by solving mathematics problems rather than completing drills for basic skills development.

Teaching for understanding requires carefully designed tasks. Homework assignments should have clear criteria and/or written rubrics that describe expectations and establish student goals. The teacher must be certain that students have access to the materials and resources they will need to complete the assignment. Teachers should examine all student work.

Homework assignments must be purposeful. Some legitimate purposes for homework include introducing new content, elaborating on information that has already been addressed to deepen students' knowledge, and providing opportunities for students to explore topics of their own interest.

Less is often more when it comes to homework. A product that has been refined by the student results in more effective learning than a large volume of work completed with little thought. The quality of student work is often determined by the standards a teacher sets on the assignment, time spent reviewing the expectations, and suggestions for improvements. Selling students on the importance of an assignment as a learning event is important: their ownership will determine the depth and breadth of their learning.

Resources for Learning More

American Association for the Advancement of Science, Project 2061. (1993). Benchmarks for science literacy.

Baker, D., & LeTendre, G. (2005). National differences, global similarities.

Kieff, J. (2004). Classroom idea-sparkers.

Loveless, T. (2004). How well are Americans learning?

Marzano, R. J., & Kendall, J. S. (1996). A comprehensive guide to designing standards-based districts, schools, and classrooms.

Marzano, R. J., & Pickering, D. J. (2007, March). The case for and against homework.

Marzano, R. J., Pickering, D. J., & Pollock, J. E. (2001). Classroom instruction that works.

National Council of Teachers of Mathematics. (2000). Principles and standards for school mathematics.

National Science Foundation. (1999). Inquiry thoughts, views, and strategies for the K–5 classroom.

For All

Teaching

Assessment

Curriculum

Technology

Learning

What is the impact of teacher learning on student learning?

"Teachers need to understand the big ideas of mathematics and be able to represent mathematics as a coherent and connected enterprise. Their decisions and their actions in the classroom—all of which affect how well their students learn mathematics—should be based on this knowledge."

–National Council of Teachers of Mathematics, 2000, p. 17.

Research and Ideas to Know About

One of the strongest predictors of students' success is the quality of their teacher. Highly qualified teachers with both mathematics content knowledge and pedagogical skills are more effective. Teachers who continue to learn deepen their understanding of content applications and knowledge, effective instructional strategies, theoretical bases for instructional decisions, and confidence in decision making. They are more likely to become reflective, competent, professional teachers.

Mathematics teachers who lead students to explore ideas, pose conjectures, and explain their reasoning need robust understanding of the subject. Teachers who use a more inquiry-based approach and who create learning communities need a deep, connected understanding of mathematical concepts in order to facilitate student learning. Comfortable with their own understanding, they can anticipate and respond to student misconceptions as well as student insights. Without this understanding, teachers are limited by their own misconceptions, often the same ones entertained by their students. Furthermore, to select mathematical tasks that enable all students to grow mathematically, they need a deep sense of how each task relates to other tasks, to prior learning, and to future concepts.

Many studies have explored teacher knowledge as evidenced in mathematics achievement tests and formal coursework. More recent studies connect a teacher's knowledge of mathematics and ability to teach mathematics effectively with student achievement. Critical teacher characteristics and behaviors are

- Well-defined vision of quality mathematics and reflective classroom practices.
- Deep understanding of mathematics—concepts, practices, principles, representations, and applications.
- Deep understanding of the ways children learn mathematics.
- Implementation of methods that draw out and build upon student mathematical thinking.
- Continual engagement in reflective practice.
- Sustained focus on student learning.

The Teaching Principle of the NCTM *Principles and Standards for School Mathematics* emphasizes the importance of teacher preparation and continual professional growth for achieving student understanding of mathematics.

Implications to Think About

A community of learners includes a teacher who is a learner with students. Mathematics education standards that establish learning goals for students should, and do, expect as much of teachers. When teachers have a deep understanding about the subject matter, they better anticipate and overcome student mathematics misconceptions, and they become more confident about teaching in an inquiry mode. A job-embedded opportunity for such learning occurs while teaching a rich, conceptually-based mathematics program. Teachers become both students and teachers of the content. A broad understanding of mathematics provides teachers with one of the key components for the integration of the various strands of mathematics as well as integration across the curriculum.

Teachers should make decisions based upon data; the best data source is the information they gather in the classroom. Teachers who are learners engage in action research to hone their instructional decision-making skills. They use the data they collect to adjust their instruction. Teachers and leaders of mathematics instruction should allow time for teachers to practice and reflect on various methods for teaching and representing mathematics content.

Mathematics teachers should stay current in mathematics as well as mathematics education. One way professional teachers maintain a current knowledge of their content area is through memberships in professional organizations. These organizations provide journals that synthesize current topics in mathematics and mathematics education.

Perhaps the most significant result of teachers being engaged in learning is the enthusiasm for learning they bring to the classroom. Students know when a teacher is excited about learning. This adds to students' interest and enthusiasm for learning.

Resources for Learning More

Cady, J., Meier, S., & Lubinski, C. (2006, May–June). Developing mathematics teachers.

Darling-Hammond, L. & Ball, D. L. (2000). Teaching for high standards.

Johnson, J. (2000). Teaching and learning mathematics.

Ma, L. (1999). Knowing and teaching elementary mathematics.

National Council of Teachers of Mathematics. (2000). Principles and standards for school mathematics.

National Council of Supervisors of Mathematics. (2007, September). Improving student achievement by leading sustained professional learning for mathematics content and pedagogical knowledge development.

Wenglinsky, H. (2000). How teaching matters.

For All

Teaching

Assessment

Curriculum

Technology

Learning

Bibliography

American Association for the Advancement of Science, Project 2061. (1993). *Benchmarks for science literacy.* New York: Oxford University Press.

American Psychological Association (APA). (1997). *Learner-centered psychological principles.* Retrieved January 23, 2002, from http://www.apa.org/ ed/lcp2/lcp14.html

Anderson, R. C., Hiebert, E. H., Scott, J. A., & Wilkinson, I. A. G. (1984). *Becoming a nation of readers: The report of The Commission on Reading.* Washington, DC: The National Institute of Education.

Apthorp, H. S., Bodrova, E., Dean, C. B., & Florian, J. E. (2001). *Noteworthy perspectives: Teaching to the core–Reading, writing, and mathematics.* Aurora, CO: Mid-continent Research for Education and Learning.

Armstrong, T. (1994). *Multiple intelligences in the classroom.* Alexandria, VA: Association for Supervision and Curriculum Development.

Armstrong, T. (1998). *Awakening genius in the classroom.* Alexandria, VA: Association for Supervision and Curriculum Development.

Bailey, T. (1997). Integrating vocational and academic education. In *High school mathematics at work: Essays and examples for the education of all students* (pp. 24–29). Washington, DC: The National Academies Press.

Baker, D., & LeTendre, G. (2005). *National differences, global similarities: World culture and the future of schooling.* Palo Alto, CA: Stanford University Press.

Ball, D.L, Lubienski, S. & Mewborn, D. (2001). Research on teaching mathematics: The unsolved problem of teachers' mathematical knowledge. In V. Richardson (Ed.), *Handbook of Research on Teaching* (4th ed.). New York: Macmillan.

Banilower, E. R., Boyd, S. E., Pasley, J. D., & Weiss, I. R. (2006). *Lessons from a decade of mathematics and science reform: A capstone report for the local systemic change through teacher enhancement initiative.* Chapel Hill, NC: Horizon Research, Inc.

Barber, M. and Mourshed, M. (2007). *How the world's best performing education systems come out on top.* London: McKinsey and Company.

Barton, M. L., & Heidema, C. (2002). *Teaching reading in mathematics.* (2nd ed.). Aurora, CO: Mid-continent Research for Education and Learning.

Bass, H. (2003, Feb.) Computational fluency, algorithms, and mathematical proficiency: One mathematician's perspective. Teaching Children Mathematics, 9 (6), 322–327.

Battista, M. T. (1994). Teacher beliefs and the reform movement in mathematics education. *Phi Delta Kappan, 75*(6), 462.

Beck, S. (2007, August). *The good, the bad and the ugly: Or, why it's a good idea to evaluate web sources.* [Web site]. http://lib.nmsu.edu/instruction/eval.html

Billmeyer, R., & Barton, M. L. (2002). *Teaching reading in the content areas* (2nd ed.). Aurora, CO: Mid-continent Research for Education and Learning.

Black, P. (2003). *Assessment for learning.* Maidenhead, England: Open University Press.

Blakey, E., & Spence, S. (1990). *Developing metacognition.* Syracuse, NY: ERIC Clearinghouse on Information Resources for Learning More. (ERIC Document Reproduction Service No. ED327218).

Blythe, T., Allen, D. & Powell, B. S. (1999) *Looking together at student work: A companion to assessing student learning.* New York: Teachers College Press.

Boaler, J. (1997). *Experiencing school mathematics: Teaching styles, sex, and setting.* Buckingham, UK: Open University Press.

Bransford, J. D., Brown, A. L., & Cocking, R. R. (Eds.). (2000). *How people learn: Brain, mind, experience, and school: Expanded edition.* Washington, DC: The National Academies Press.

Bright, G. W. & Joyner, J. N. (Eds.). (1998). *Classroom assessment in mathematics: Views from a National Science Foundation working conference.* New York: University Press of America.

Brooks, J. G., & Brooks, M. G. (1993). *In search of understanding: The case for constructivist classrooms.* Alexandria, VA: Association for Supervision and Curriculum Development.

Brown, J., Collins, A., & Duguid, P. (1989). Situated cognition and the culture of learning. *Educational Researcher, 18,* 32–42.

Buehl, D. (1998). Making math make sense: Tactics help kids understand math language. *WEAC News and Views, 34*(3), 17.

Burke, M. J., & Curcio, F. R. (Eds.). (2000). *Learning mathematics for a new century. 2000 yearbook.* Reston, VA: National Council of Teachers of Mathematics.

Burke, K., & Dunn, R. (2002, Spring). Teaching math effectively to elementary students. *Academic Exchange Quarterly, 6*(1).

Burns, M. (1995). *Writing in math class: A resource for grades 2–8.* Sausalito, CA: Math Solutions.

Burns, M. (2007). *About teaching mathematics: A K–8 resource* (3rd ed.). White Plains, NY: Math Solutions Publications.

Bibliography

Bush, W. S., & Greer, A. S. (Eds.). (1999). *Mathematics assessment: A practical handbook for grades 9–12.* Reston, VA: National Council of Teachers of Mathematics.

Bush, W. S., Leinwand, S., & Beck, P. (Eds.). (2000). *Mathematics assessment: A practical handbook for grades 6–8.* Reston, VA: National Council of Teachers of Mathematics.

Cady, J., Meier, S., & Lubinski, C. (2006, May-June). Developing mathematics teachers: The transition from preservice to experienced teacher. *Journal of Educational Research, 99*(5), 295–305.

Caine, R. N., & Caine, G. (1994). *Making connections: Teaching and the human brain.* Menlo Park, CA: Addison-Wesley.

Campbell, P. (1992). *Math, science, and your daughter: What can parents do? Encouraging girls in math and science series.* Washington, DC: Office of Educational Research and Improvement, U.S. Department of Education.

Campbell, P., & Kreinberg, N. (1998). *Moving into the mainstream: From equity as a separate concept to high quality includes all.* Washington, DC: National Science Foundation. Collaboration for Equity Fairness in Science and Mathematics Education. Retrieved 4/22/08 from http://www. campbell-kibler.com/Moving_to_Mainstream.htm

Carpenter, T. P., Fenneman, E., Franke, M. L., Levi, L., & Empson, S. B. (1999). *Children's mathematics: Cognitively guided instruction.* Portsmouth, NH: Heinemann.

Carpenter, T. P., Levi, L., & Farnsworth, V. (2000, Fall). Building a foundation for learning algebra in the elementary grades. *inBrief: K–12 mathematics & science research & implications for policymakers, educators & researchers seeking to improve student learning & achievement 1*(2).

Carroll, W., & Porter, D. (1998). Alternative algorithms for whole-number operations. In L. J. Morrow (Ed.), *The teaching and learning of algorithms in school mathematics. 1998 yearbook* (pp. 106–114). Reston, VA: National Council of Teachers of Mathematics.

Cawelti, G. (Ed.). (2004). *Handbook of research on improving student achievement* (3rd ed.). Alexandria, VA: Educational Research Service.

Chapin, S. H., O'Connor, C., & Anderson, N. C. Classroom. (2003). *Discussions: Using math talk to help students learn, grades 1–6.* Sausalito, CA: Math Solutions Professional Development.

Charles, R. I. (2005, Summer). Big ideas and understandings as the foundation for elementary and middle school mathematics. *Journal of Mathematics Education Leadership (7)*3, 9–16.

Chicago Lesson Study Group. http://www.lessonstudygroup.net/

Clarke, D. (1997). *Constructive assessment in mathematics: Practical steps for classroom teachers.* Berkeley, CA: Key Curriculum Press.

Colburn, W. (1821). *Intellectual arithmetic, upon the inductive method of instruction. Boston MA: Reynolds & Co. Boston.*

Collins, A. M. (2000). Yours is not to reason why, just plug in the numbers and multiply. *Education Week, 20*(1), 62.

Compass Learning. Professional development [Web site]. http://www.compasslearning.com/services/Development.aspx

Cuoco, A. A. (Ed.). (2001). *The roles of representation in school mathematics. 2001 yearbook.* Reston, VA: National Council of Teachers of Mathematics.

Darling-Hammond, L. & Ball, D. L. (2000). *Teaching for high standards: What policymakers need to know and be able to do.* (CPRE paper. No. JRE-04). Philadelphia, PA: University of Pennsylvania, Consortium for Policy Research in Education.

Darling-Hammond, L. (1997). *The right to learn: A blueprint for creating schools that work.* San Francisco, CA: Jossey-Bass.

DeCorte, E. Greer, B., & Verschaffel, L. (1996). Mathematics teaching and learning. In D. C. Berliner & R. C. Calfee (Eds.), *Handbook of educational psychology* (pp. 491–549). New York: Macmillan.

Dogan-Dunlap, H. (2004). *Changing students' perception of mathematics through an integrated, collaborative, field-based approach to teaching and learning mathematics.* Paper presented at the Joint Mathematics Meetings of the AMS/MAA, Phoenix, AZ.

Dowker, A. (1992). Computational strategies of professional mathematicians. *Journal for Research in Mathematics Education, 23*(1), 4–55.

Driscoll, M. (1999). Fostering algebraic thinking: A guide for teachers, grades 6-10. Portsmouth, NH: Heinemann.

Driscoll, M., DiMatteo, R.W., Nikula, J. & Egan, M. (2007). Fostering geometric thinking: A guide for teachers, grades 5-10. Portsmouth, NH: Heinemann.

Duschl, R. A., Schweingruber, H. A., & Shouse, A. W. (Eds.). (2007). *Taking science to school: Learning and teaching sciences in grades K–8.* Washington, DC: National Academies Press.

Education Development Center, Inc. (2005). *The K–12 mathematics curriculum center.* [Web site]. http://www2.edc.org/mcc/

Bibliography

Equals and family math. [Web site] http://www.lhs.berkeley.edu/equals/

Evan, A., Gray, T., & Olchefske, J. (2006). *The gateway to student success in mathematics and science.* Washington, DC: American Institutes for Research.

Felder, R. (1996). Matters of style. *ASEE Prism, 6*(4), 18–23.

Fennema, E., & Romberg, T. A. (Eds.). (1999). *Mathematics classrooms that promote understanding.* Mahwah, NJ: Lawrence Erlbaum.

Fernandez, C. Lesson study research group. [Web site]. http://www.tc.edu/lessonstudy/

Fisher, D., Frey, N. (2007). *Checking for understanding: Formative assessment techniques for your classroom.* Alexandria, VA: Association for Supervision and Curriculum Development.

Forum on Education Statistics. (2002). *Technology in schools: Suggestions, tools and guidelines for assessing technology in elementary and secondary education.* Washington, DC: National Center for Education Statistics. (NCES No. 2003-313)

Foster, G., Sawicki, E., Schaeffer, H., & Zelinski, V. (2002). *I think, therefore I learn!* Ontario, Canada: Pembroke Publishers.

Frand, J. L. (2000). The information-age mindset. *Educause Review, 35*(5), 15–24.

Freer Weiss, D. M. (2006, January). Keeping it real: The rationale for using manipulatives in the middle grades. *Mathematics Teaching in the Middle School, 11*(5), 238–242.

Friedman, M. I., Harwell, D. H., & Schnepel, K. C. (2006). *Effective instruction: A handbook of evidence-based strategies.* Columbia, SC: The Institute for Evidence-Based Decision-Making in Education.

Froelich, G. (1991). Connecting mathematics. Reston, VA: National Council of Teachers of Mathematics.

Fromboluti, C. S., & Rinck, N. (1999, June). *Early childhood: Where learning begins—mathematics.* Retrieved January 24, 2008, from the U.S. Department of Education Web site: http://www.ed.gov/pubs/EarlyMath/index.html

Frykholm, J. A. (2005). Integrating mathematics and science: In D. Berlin and A. White (Eds.), *Collaboration for the improvement of science and mathematics education: A global effort. Columbus,* OH: International Consortium of Research in Mathematics and Science Education.

Fullan, M. G. (2001). *The new meaning of educational change* (3rd ed.). New York: Teachers College Press.

Fuson, K. C. (1992). Research on learning and teaching addition and subtraction of whole numbers. In G. Leinhardt, R. T. Putnam, & R. A. Hattrup (Eds.), *The analysis of arithmetic for mathematics teaching* (pp. 53–187). Hillsdale, NJ: Lawrence Erlbaum.

Gaddy, B. B., Dean, C. B., & Kendall, J. S. (2002). *Noteworthy perspectives: Keeping the focus on learning.* Aurora, CO: Mid-continent Research for Education and Learning.

Gardner, H. T. (1993). *Multiple intelligences: The theory into practice.* New York: Basic Books.

Garet, M. S., Porter, A. C., Desimone, L., & Birman, B. F. (2001). What makes professional development effective? Results from a national sample of teachers. *American Educational Research Journal, 38*(4), 915–945.

Glandfield, F., Bush, W.S., & Stenmark, J.K. (Eds.) (2003). Mathematics assessment: A practical handbook for grades K–2. Reston, VA: National Council of Teachers of Mathematics.

Glatthorn, A. (1998). *Performance assessment and standards-based curricula: The achievement cycle.* Larchmont, NY: Eye on Education.

Goldberg, P. D., & Bush, W. S. (2003, September). Using metacognitive skills to improve 3rd graders' math problem solving. *Focus on Learning Problems in Mathematics, 25*(4).

Goldsmith, L. T., Mark, J., & Kantrov, I. (2000). *Choosing a standards-based mathematics curriculum.* Portsmouth, NH: Heinemann.

Groves, S., & Stacey, K. (1998). Calculators in primary mathematics: Exploring number before teaching algorithms. In L. J. Morrow (Ed.), *The teaching and learning of algorithms in school mathematics. 1998 yearbook.* Reston, VA: National Council of Teachers of Mathematics.

Grunow, J. E. (2001). *Planning curriculum in mathematics.* Madison, WI: Wisconsin Department of Public Instruction.

Halpern, D., Aronson, J., Reimer, N., Simpkins, S. Star, J., & Wentzel, K. (2007). *Encouraging girls in math and science (NCER 2007-2003).* Washington, DC: National Center for Education Research, Institute of Education Sciences. Retrieved from the U. S. Department of Education Web site: http://ncer.ed.gov

Bibliography

Handal, B. (2003). Teachers' mathematical beliefs: A review. *The Mathematics Educator, 13*(2), 47–57.

Hellwig, S. J., Monroe, E. E., Jacobs, J. S. (2000, November). Making informed choices: Selecting children's trade books for mathematics instruction. *Teaching Children Mathematics, 7*(3), 138–43.

Hembree, R., & Dessart, D. (1986). Effects of hand held calculators in pre-college mathematics education: A meta-analysis. *Journal for Research in Mathematics Education, 17*, 83–89.

Henningsen, M., & Stein, M. (1997). Mathematical tasks and student cognition: Classroom-based factors that support and inhibit high-level mathematical thinking and reasoning. *Journal for Research in Mathematics Education, 28*(5), 524–549.

Heritage, M. (2007, October). Formative assessment: What do teachers need to know and do? *Phi Delta Kappan, 89*(2), 140–145.

Herman, J. L., & Abedi, J. (2004). *Issues in assessing English language learners' opportunity to learn mathematics* (CSE Report 633). Los Angeles, CA: Center for the Study of Evaluation, National Center for Research on Evaluation, Standards, and Student Testing, Graduate School of Education & Information Studies, University of California.

Heuser, D. (2000, January). Mathematics workshop: Mathematics class becomes learner centered. *Teaching Children Mathematics, 6*(5), 288–95.

Hiebert, J. (1999). Relationship between research and the NCTM standards. *Journal of Research in Mathematics Education, 30*(1), 3–19.

Hiebert, J., & Carpenter, T. P. (1992). Learning and teaching with understanding. In D. Grouws (Ed.). *Handbook of research on mathematics teaching and learning* (pp. 65–97). New York: Macmillan.

Hiebert, J., Carpenter, T. P., Fennema, E., Fuson, K. C., Kearne, D., Murray, H., Olivier, A., & Human, P. (1997). *Making sense: Teaching and learning mathematics with understanding.* Portsmouth, NH: Heinemann.

Hill, H. C., Rowan, B., & Loewenberg Ball, D. (2005). Effects of teachers' mathematical knowledge for teaching on student achievement. *American Educational Research Journal, 42*(2), 371–406.

Hirsch, C. R. (2007). (Ed.) *Perspectives on design and development of school mathematics curricula.* Reston, VA: National Council of Teachers of Mathematics.

Hirsch, C., Cox, D., Kasmar, L., Madden, S. & Moore, D. (2007, February). Some common themes and notable differences across recent national mathematics curriculum documents. In *K–12 Mathematics: What Should Students Learn and When Should They Learn It? Conference Proceedings* (pp.40–51). Arlington, VA: Center for the Study of Mathematics Curriculum.

Hoachlander, G. (1997). Organizing mathematics education around work. In L. Steen (Ed.), *Why numbers count: Quantitative literacy for tomorrow's America* (pp. 122–136). New York: College Board.

Horton, R. M., Hedetniemi, T., Wiegert, E., & Wagner, J. R. (2006, April). Integrating curriculum through themes. *Mathematics Teaching in the Middle School (11)*8, 408–414.

Hudson, P., & Miller, S. (2005). *Designing and implementing mathematics instruction for students with diverse learning needs.* Boston: Allyn & Bacon, Inc.

Institute of Education Sciences. (n.d.) Fast facts. Retrieved April 28, 2008 from http://nces.ed.gov/fastfacts/display.asp?id=1

Institute of Education Sciences. *What works clearinghouse* [Web site]. http://ies.ed.gov/ncee/wwc/

International Society for Technology in Education. (2007). *National education technology standards for students: The next generation.* (2nd ed.). Eugene, OR: Author.

International Technology Education Association. (2000). *Standards for technological literacy: Content for the study of technology.* Retrieved January 24, 2002, from ITEA Web site: http://www.iteawww.org/TAA/PDF/xstnd.pdf

Jensen, E. (1998). *Teaching with the brain in mind.* Alexandria, VA: Association for Supervision and Curriculum Development.

Johnson, J. (2000). *Teaching and learning mathematics: Using research to shift from the "yesterday" mind to the "tomorrow" mind.* Olympia, WA: Resource Center, Office of the Superintendent of Public Instruction.

Kamii, C., & Dominick, A. (1998). The harmful effects of algorithms in grades 1–4. In L. Morrow (Ed.), *The teaching and learning of algorithms in school mathematics* (pp. 130–140). Reston, VA: National Council of Teachers of Mathematics.

Kathy Schrock's guide for educators. [Web site] http://school.discoveryeducation.com/schrockguide

Keleher, L. A. (2006, November). Building a career mathematics file: Challenging students to find the importance of mathematics in a variety of occupations. *Mathematics Teacher, 100*(4), 292–297.

Bibliography

Kieff, J. (2004). Classroom idea-sparkers. *Childhood education (81)*.

Kilpatrick, J., & Swafford, J. (Eds.). (2002). *Helping children learn mathematics*. Washington, DC: National Academy Press.

Kilpatrick, J., Swafford, J., & Findell, B. (Eds.). (2001). *Adding it up: Helping children learn mathematics*. Washington, DC: National Academy Press.

Kilpatrick, W., Martin, G., & Schifter, D. (Eds.). (2003). *A research companion to principles and standards for school mathematics*. Reston, VA: National Council of Teachers of Mathematics.

Kleiman, G. M. (2004). *What does the research say? Does technology combined with inquiry-based lessons increase students' learning?* Newton, MA: Education Development Center.

Kulm, G., Roseman, J. E., Treistman, M. (1999). A benchmarks-based approach to textbook evaluation. *Science Books & Films, 35*(4).

Land, S. M., & Greene, B. A. (2000). Project-based learning with the World Wide Web: A qualitative study of resource integration. *Educational Technology Research and Development, 48*(1), 45–67.

Lawrenz, F. Gravely, A., & Ooms, A. (2006, March). Perceived helpfulness and amount of use of technology in science and mathematics classes at different grade levels. *School Science and Mathematics, 106*(3), 133.

Lazear, D. (2004). *Higher order thinking: The multiple intelligences way*. Chicago, IL: Zephyr Press.

Leinhardt, G., Zaslavsky, O., & Stein, M. K. (1990). Functions, graphs, and graphing: Tasks, learning, and teaching. *Review of Educational Research, 60*(1), 1–64.

Lester, F. K., Jr. (Ed.) (2007). *Second handbook of research on mathematics teaching and learning*. Charlotte, NC: Information Age Publishing.

Loucks-Horsley, S., Hewson, P. W., Love, N., & Stiles, K. (Eds.). (1998). *Designing professional development for teachers of science and mathematics*. Thousand Oaks, CA: Corwin Press.

Loveless, T. (2004). *How well are American students learning? With studies of NAEP math items, middle school math teachers, and the revamped Blue Ribbon Schools Awards (1)*5, Washington DC: The Brookings Institution.

Luft, P., Brown, C. M., & Sutherin, L. J. (2007, July) Are you and your students bored with the benchmarks? Sinking under the standards? Then transform your teaching through transition! *Teaching Exceptional Children, 39*(6), 39–46.

Ma, L. (1999). *Knowing and teaching elementary mathematics: Teachers' understanding of fundamental mathematics in China and the United States*. Mahwah, NJ: Lawrence Erlbaum.

Marzano, R. J. (2004). *Building background knowledge for academic achievement: Research on what works in schools*. Alexandria, VA: Association for Supervision and Curriculum Development.

Marzano, R. J. (2003). *What works in schools*. Alexandria, VA: Association for Supervision and Curriculum Development.

Marzano, R. J., & Kendall, J. S. (1996). *A comprehensive guide to designing standards-based districts, schools, and classrooms*. Alexandria, VA: Association for Supervision and Curriculum Development.

Marzano, R. J., Norford, J. S., Paynter, D. E., Pickering, D. J., & Gaddy, B. B. (2001). *A handbook for classroom instruction that works*. Alexandria, VA: Association for Supervision and Curriculum Development.

Marzano, R. J., & Pickering, D. J. (2007, March). The case for and against homework. *Educational Leadership (64)*6, 74–79.

Marzano, R. J., Pickering, D. J., & Pollock, J. E. (2001). *Classroom instruction that works: Research-based strategies for increasing student achievement*. Alexandria, VA: Association for Supervision and Curriculum Development.

Maynard, S., & Howley, A. (June 1997). *Parent and community involvement in rural schools*. ERIC Clearinghouse on Rural Education and Small Schools. (ERIC Document Reproduction Service No EDO-RC-97-3).

McKeachie, W. J. (1995, November). Learning styles can become learning strategies. *The National Teaching & Learning Forum, 4*(6). Retrieved January 24, 2002, from http://www.ntlf.com/html/pi/9511/article1.htm

McMillan, J. (Ed.). (2007). *Formative classroom assessment: Theory into practice*. New York: Teachers College Press.

Meier, D. (1995). *The power of their ideas: Lessons for America from a small school in Harlem*. Boston, MA: Beacon Press.

Mewborn, D. S. (2003). Teachers, teacher knowledge, and their professional development. In W. Kilpatrick, G. Martin, & D. Schifter (Eds.), *A research companion to principles and standards for school mathematics*. Reston, VA: National Council of Teachers of Mathematics.

Mid-continent Research for Education and Learning. (2005). *McREL Insights: Professional development analysis*. Aurora, CO: Author.

Bibliography

Mid-continent Research for Education and Learning. (2005). *McREL Insights: Standards-based education: Putting research into practice.* Aurora, CO: Author.

Middleton, J. A., & Spanias, P. (1999). Motivation for achievement in mathematics: Findings, generalizations, and criticisms of the recent research. *Journal for Research in Mathematics Education, 30*(1), 65–88.

Mirra, A. (2003). *Administrator's guide: How to support and improve mathematics education in your school.* Reston, VA: National Council of Teachers of Mathematics.

Mirra, A. (Ed.). (2004). *A family's guide: Fostering your child's success in school mathematics.* Reston, VA: National Council of Teachers of Mathematics.

Mistretta, R. (2005). Integrating technology into the mathematics classroom: The role of teacher preparation programs. *The Mathematics Educator, 15*(1), 18–24.

Mokros, J., Russell, S. J., & Economopoulos, K. (1995). *Beyond arithmetic: Changing mathematics in the elementary classroom.* Palo Alto, CA: Dale Seymour.

Morge, S. P. (2007, August). Eliciting students' beliefs about who is good at mathematics. *Mathematics Teacher, 101*(1), 50–55.

Moschkovich, J., & Schoenfeld, A. H. (1993). Aspects of understanding: On multiple perspectives and representation of linear relations and connections among them. In T. A. Romberg, E. Fennema, & T. P. Carpenter (Eds.), *Integrating research on the graphical representation of functions* (pp. 69–100). Hillsdale, NJ: Lawrence Erlbaum.

Moses, R. P., & Cobb, C. E., Jr. (2001). *Radical equations: Math literacy and civil rights.* Boston, MA: Beacon Press.

Moyer, P. S., Bolyard, J. J., & Spikell, M. A. (2002, February). What are virtual manipulatives? *Teaching Children Mathematics, 8*(6), 372.

National Academy of Sciences. (1996). *Renewing U.S. mathematics.* Overhead package for *Curriculum and Evaluation Standards for School Mathematics 1989.* Reston, VA: National Council of Teachers of Mathematics.

National Center for Education Statistics. (2000). *Pursuing excellence: Comparison of 8th grade mathematics and science achievement from a U.S. perspective, 1985 and 1999.* Washington, DC: U. S. Government Printing Office.

National Commission on Excellence in Education. (1983). *A Nation at risk: The imperative for educational reform.* Washington, DC: U.S. Government Printing Office.

National Commission on Mathematics and Science Teaching for the 21st Century. (2000). *Before it's too late: A report to the nation from the National Commission on Mathematics and Science Teaching for the 21st Century.* Washington, DC: U.S. Department of Education.

National Council of Supervisors of Mathematics. (2007, September). *Improving student achievement by leading sustained professional learning for mathematics content and pedagogical knowledge development.* Denver, CO: Author.

National Council of Teachers of Mathematics. (1995). *Assessment standards for school mathematics.* Reston, VA: Author.

National Council of Teachers of Mathematics. (2005, May). *Computation, calculators, and common sense: A position of the National Council of Teachers of Mathematics.* Retrieved January 23, 2008, from the National Council of Teachers of Mathematics Web site: http://www.nctm.org/uploadedFiles/About_NCTM/Position_Statements/computation.pdf

National Council of Teachers of Mathematics. (1989). *Curriculum and evaluation standards for school mathematics.* Reston, VA: Author.

National Council of Teachers of Mathematics. (2006). *Curriculum focal points for pre-kindergarten through grade 8 mathematics: A quest for coherence.* Reston, VA: Author.

National Council of Teachers of Mathematics. (1999). *Figure this! Math challenges for families, helping your child learn math.* [Web site]. http://www.figurethis.org/

National Council of Teachers of Mathematics. (2007). *Mathematics teaching today: Improving practice, improving student learning.* Reston, VA: Author.

National Council of Teachers of Mathematics. (2008). *The role of technology in the learning and teaching of mathematics: Position statement.* Retrieved April 23, 2008, from the National Council of Teachers of Mathematics Web site: http://nctm.org/about/content.aspx?id=14233

National Council of Teachers of Mathematics. (2000). *Principles and standards for school mathematics.* Reston, VA: Author.

National Library of Vurtual Manipulatives [Web site] http://nlvm.usu.edu

National Mathematics Advisory Panel. (2008). *Foundations for success: The final report of The National Mathematics Advisory Panel.* Washington, DC: Author.

National Mathematics Advisory Panel. (2008). *Report of the Task Group on Learning Processes.* Washington, DC: Author.

Bibliography

National Parent Teacher Association. (2004). *National standards for parent/family involvement programs.* Bloomington, IN: Solution Tree.

National Research Council. (1999). *Designing mathematics or science curriculum programs: A guide for using mathematics and science education standards.* Washington, DC: National Academy Press.

National Research Council (2003). *Engaging schools: Fostering high school students' motivation to learn.* Washington, DC: The National Academies Press.

National Research Council. (1989). *Everybody counts: A report to the nation on the future of mathematics education.* Washington, DC: National Academy Press.

National Science Board. (2008). *Science and engineering indicators 2008.* (Vols. 1–2). Arlington, VA: National Science Foundation.

National Science Foundation. (1999). Inquiry thoughts, views, and strategies for the K–5 classroom. *(Foundations: A monograph for professionals in science, mathematics, and technology education, 2,* No. NSF 99–148). Arlington, VA: Author.

North Central Regional Educational Laboratory. (2004). *Connecting with the learner: An equity toolkit.* [CD-ROM]. Naperville, IL: Learning Point Associates.

North Central Regional Educational Laboratory. (2005). *Critical Issue: Mathematics education in the era of NCLB—Principles and standards.* Retrieved January 18, 2008 from North Central Regional Educational Laboratory Web site: http://www.ncrel.org/sdrs/areas/issues/content/cntareas/math/ma500.htm.

North Central Regional Educational Laboratory. (2005). *Critical Issue: Remembering the child: On equity and inclusion in mathematics and science classrooms.* Retrieved January 18, 2008, from North Central Regional Educational Laboratory Web site: http://www.ncrel.org/sdrs/areas/issues/content/cntareas/math/ma800.htm

North Central Regional Educational Laboratory. (2005). *Critical Issue: Using technology to improve student achievement.* Retrieved January 18, 2008 from North Central Regional Educational Laboratory Web site: http://www.ncrel.org/sdrs/areas/issues/methods/technlgy/te800.htm

Oakes, J. (2005). *Keeping track: How schools structure inequality* (2nd ed.). Yale University Press.

Oberer, J. J. (2003, Spring). Effects of learning-style teaching on elementary students' behaviors, achievement, and attitudes. *Academic Exchange Quarterly, 7.*

O'Donnell, B. D. (2001, April). A personal journey: Integrating mathematics and service learning. *Mathematics Teaching in the Middle School, 6*(8), 440–46.

Oliva, M. (2005). *NCLB implementation center, building capacity through high-quality teachers: A literature review on recruiting and retaining high-quality teachers.* Naperville, IL: Learning Point Associates.

Olson, S. & Loucks-Horsley, S. (Eds.). (2000). *Inquiry and the national science education standards: A guide for teaching and learning.* Washington, DC: The National Academies Press.

Parker, R. (2006). *Supporting school mathematics: How to work with parents and the public.* Portsmouth, NH: Heinemann.

Pashler, H., Bain, P., Bottge, B., Graesser, A., Koedinger, K., McDaniel, M., & Metcalfe, J. (2007). *Organizing instruction and study to improve student learning: A Practice Guide* (NCER 2007–2004). Washington, DC: National Center for Education Research, Institute of Education Sciences, U. S. Department of Education. Retrieved from http://ies.ed.gov/ncee/wwc/practiceguides/index.asp

Payne, R. K. (2005). *A framework for understanding poverty.* (Rev. ed.). Highlands, TX: aha! Process, Inc.

PBS TeacherLine. (n.d.). *Developing mathematical thinking with effective questions.* Retrieved from http://teacherline.pbs.org/teacherline/resources/questionsheet_vma.pdf

Philipp, R. A. (2007). Mathematics teachers' beliefs and affect. In F. Lester (Ed.), *Second handbook of research on mathematics teaching and learning* (pp. 257-315). Reston, VA: National Council of Teachers of Mathematics.

Phye, G. (Ed.) (1997). *Handbook of academic learning: Construction of knowledge.* New York: Academic Press.

Pitler, H., Hubbell, E. R., Kuhn, M., & Malenoski, K. (2007). *Using technology with classroom instruction that works.* Alexandria, VA: Association for Supervision and Curriculum Development.

Popham, W. J. (2007). *Classroom assessment: What teachers need to know* (5th ed.). Boston: Allyn & Bacon, Inc.

Pugalee, D. K. (2004, March). A comparison of verbal and written descriptions of students' problem solving processes. *Educational Studies in Mathematics, 55*(1–3), 27–47.

Quiroz, P. A., Secada, W. G. (2003). Responding to diversity. In Gamoran, A., Anderson, C., Quiroz, P., Secada, W., Williams, T., & Ashman, S. *Transforming teaching in math and science: How schools and districts can support change.* New York: Teachers College Press.

Bibliography

Remillard, J. T., & Jackson, K. (2006). Old math, new math: Parents' experiences with standards-based reform. *Mathematical Thinking & Learning: An International Journal, 8*(3), 231–259.

Richard-Amato, P. A. Snow, M. A. (Eds.). (2005) *Academic success for English language learners: Strategies for K–12 mainstream teachers.* Upper Saddle River, NJ: Pearson Education.

Rigelman, N. (2007, February). Fostering mathematical thinking and problem solving: The teacher's role. *Teaching Children Mathematics, 13*(6), 308.

Roempler, K. S. (2002, July). Search smarter. In Thorson, A. (Ed.), Increasing your mathematics and science content knowledge. *ENC Focus 9*(3).

Romagnano, L. (2006). Mathematics assessment literacy: Concepts and terms in large-scale assessment. Reston, VA: National Council of Teachers of Mathematics.

Romberg, T., & Kaput, J. (1999). Mathematics worth teaching, mathematics worth understanding. In E. Fenema & T. Romberg (Eds.), *Mathematics classrooms that promote understanding* (pp. 3–17). Mahwah, NJ: Lawrence Erlbaum.

Ronis, D. (2006). *Brain-compatible mathematics* (2nd ed.). Thousand Oaks, CA: Corwin Press.

Schackow, J. B., & Thompson, D. R. (2005, September). High school students' attitudes toward mathematics. *Academic exchange quarterly.*

Schackow, J. B. (2006). Using virtual manipulatives to model computation with fractions. *On-Math Articles.* Retrieved January 23, 2008, from http://my.nctm.org/eresources/toc_onmath.asp?journal_id=6

Schmidt, M.E. & Vandewater, E.A. (2008, Spring). Media and attention, cognition, and school achievement. Future of Children, 18(1), 63–85.

Schmidt, W., Houang, R., & Cogan, L. (2002, Summer). A coherent curriculum: The case of mathematics. *American Educator, 26*(2), 10-26.

Schmidt, W., & Valverde, G. (1998). Refocusing U.S. math and science education. *Issues in Science and Technology, 14*(2), 60–66.

Schneider, M. (2007). *NAEP–The nation's report card: Mathematics 2007.* Retrieved January 18, 2008, from http://nationsreportcard.gov/math_2007

Schoenfeld, A. H. (2002, Jan/Feb). Making mathematics work for all children: Issues of standards, testing, and equity. *Educational Researcher, 31*(1), 13–25.

Schoenfeld, A. H. (2004, January & March) The math wars. *Educational Policy 18*(1), 253–286.

Schwartz, S. L. (2007). *Teaching young children mathematics.* West Port, CT: Greenwood Publishing Group, Inc.

Seki, J. M", & Menon, R. (2007, February). Incorporating mathematics into the science program of students labeled "at-risk. School *Science and Mathematics, 107*(2), 61.

Senk, S. L., Thompson, D. R. (Eds.). (2003). Standards-based school mathematics curricula: *What are they? What do students learn?* Mahwah, NJ: Lawrence E. Erlbaum Associates.

Shafer, M., & Romberg, T. A. (1999) Assessment in classrooms that promote understanding. In E. Fennema & T. A. Romberg (Eds.), *Mathematics classrooms that promote understanding* (pp. 159-184). Mahwah, NJ: Lawrence Erlbaum.

Silver, H. F., Strong, R. W., & Perini, M. (2000). *So each may learn: Integrating learning styles and multiple intelligences.* Alexandria, VA: Association for Supervision and Curriculum Development.

Sleeter, C. E., (2005.). *Un-standardizing curriculum: Multicultural Teaching in the Standards-Based Classroom.* New York: Teachers College Press.

Smith, M. S. (2001). *Practice-based professional development for teachers of mathematics.* Reston, VA: National Council Teachers of Mathematics.

Sousa, D. A. (2005). *How the brain learns* (3rd ed.). Thousand Oaks, CA: Corwin Press.

Sousa, D. A. (2007). *How the brain learns mathematics.* Thousand Oaks, CA: Corwin Press.

Sowell, E. J. (1989). Effects of manipulative materials in mathematics instruction. J*ournal for Research in Mathematics Education, 20*(5), 498–505.

Sparks, D., & Hirsh, S. (1997). *A new vision for staff development.* Alexandria, VA: Association for Supervision and Curriculum Development.

Spoon, J., & Schell, J. (1998). Aligning student learning styles with instructor teaching styles. *Journal of Industrial Teacher Education, 35*(2). Retrieved January 24, 2002, from http://scholar.lib.vt.edu/ejournals/JITE/v35n2/spoon.html

Sprenger, M. (2003). *Differentiation through learning styles and memory.* Thousand Oaks, CA: Corwin Press.

Bibliography

Sprenger, M. (1999). *Learning and memory: The brain in action.* Alexandria, VA: Association for Supervision and Curriculum Development.

Steen, L. A. (1990). *On the shoulders of giants: New approaches to numeracy.* Washington, DC: National Academy Press.

Steffe, L. P., & Wiegel, H. G. (1996). On the nature of a model of mathematical learning. In L. P. Steffe, P. Nesher, P. Cobb, G. A. Goldin, & B. Greer (Eds.), *Theories of mathematical learning* (pp. 477–498). Mahwah, NJ: Lawrence Erlbaum.

Stein, M. K., Remillard, J., & Smith, M. S. (2007). How curriculum influences student learning. In F. Lester (Ed.), *Second handbook of research on mathematics teaching and learning.* Greenwich, CT: Information Age Publishing.

Stenmark, J. K. (1989). *Assessment alternatives in mathematics: An overview of assessment techniques that promote learning.* Berkeley, CA: University of California Regents.

Stenmark, J.K., Bush, W.S., & Allen, C. (Eds.) (2001). Mathematics assessment: A practical handbook for grades 3–5. Reston, VA: National Council of Teachers of Mathematics.

Stepanek, J., & Jarrett, D. (1997). *Assessment strategies to inform science and mathematics instruction. It's just good teaching series.* Portland, OR: Northwest Regional Educational Laboratory.

Stiggins, R. (2004). *Student-involved assessment FOR learning* (4th ed.). Upper Saddle River, NJ: Prentice-Hall, Inc.

Stiggins, R. (2005, December). From formative assessment to assessment for learning: A path to success in standards-based schools. *Phi Delta Kappan, 87*(4), 324–328.

Stigler, J. W., & Hiebert, J. (1999). *The teaching gap: Best ideas from the world's teachers for improving education in the classroom.* New York: The Free Press.

Stigler, J. W., & Hiebert, J. (2004). Improving mathematics teaching. *Educational Leadership, 61*(5), 12–17.

Suh, J., & Moyer, P. S. (2007, April). Developing students' representational fluency using virtual and physical algebra balances. *Journal of Computers in Mathematics and Science Teaching, 26*(2), 155–173.

Sullivan, P. & Lilburn, P. (2002). *Good questions for math teaching: Why ask them and what to ask.* Sausalito, CA: Math Solutions Publications.

Svedkauskaite, A., McNabb, M. (2005). *Critical issue: Multiple dimensions of assessment that support student progress in science and mathematics.* Retrieved January 18, 2008 from North Central Regional Educational Laboratory Web site: http://www.ncrel.org/sdrs/areas/issues/content/cntareas/science/sc700.htm

Sylwester, R. (1995). *A celebration of neurons: An educator's guide to the human brain.* Alexandria, VA: Association for Supervision and Curriculum Development.

Tarr, J., Reys, B., Barker, D. D., & Billstein, R. (2006, August). Selecting high-quality mathematics textbooks. *Mathematics Teaching in the Middle School, 12*(1), 50.

Tennison, A. D. (2007, August). Promoting equity in mathematics: One teacher's journey. *Mathematics Teacher, 101*(1), 28–31.

The algebra project. [Web site] http://www.algebra.org/

Thompson, C., & Zeuli, J. (1999). The frame and the tapestry: Standards-based reform and professional development. In L. Darling-Hammond & G. Sykes (Eds.), *Teaching as the learning profession: Handbook of policy and practice* (pp. 341–375). San Francisco: Jossey-Bass.

Tomlinson, C. A. (1999). *The differentiated classroom: Responding to the needs of all learners.* Alexandria, VA: Association for Supervision and Curriculum Development.

Tomlinson, C. A. (2003). *Fulfilling the promise of the differentiated classroom: Strategies and tools for responsive teaching.* Alexandria, VA: Association for Supervision and Curriculum Development.

Tomlinson, C. A., & McTighe, J. (2006). *Integrating differentiated instruction and understanding by design: Connecting content and kids.* Alexandria, VA: Association for Supervision and Curriculum Development.

Trammel, B. (2001). *Integrated mathematics? Yes, but teachers need support!* Retrieved January 23, 2008, from the National Council of Teachers of English Web site: http://www.nctm.org/resources/content.aspx?id=1712

Urquhart, V. A. & McIver, M. C. (2005). *Teaching writing in the content areas.* Alexandria, VA: Association for Supervision and Curriculum Development.

U. S. Department of Education. (2004, March). *Fact sheet: New no child left behind flexibility: Highly qualified teachers.* Retrieved from http://www.ed.gov/nclb/methods/teachers/hqtflexibility.pdf

Van't Hooft, M. & Swan, K. (Eds.). (2006). *Ubiquitous computing in education.* Mahwah, NJ: Lawrence Erlbaum Associates.

Wallace, F. H., Clark, K. K., & Cherry, M. L. (2006, September). How come? What if? So What? Reading in the mathematics classroom. *Mathematics Teaching in the Middle School, 12*(2), 108–115.

Bibliography

Walsh, J. A., & Sattes, B. D. (2005). *Quality questioning: Research-based practices to engage every learner.* Thousand Oaks, CA: Corwin Press.

Wenglinsky, H. (2000). *How teaching matters: Bringing the classroom back into discussions of teacher quality. Princeton,* NJ: Milken Family Foundation.

Westwater, A., & Wolfe, P. (2000). The brain-compatible curriculum. *Educational Leadership, 58*(3), 49–52.

Williams, D. (2007, April 2007). The what, why, and how of contextual teaching in a mathematics classroom. *Mathematics Teacher 100*(8), 572–575.

Willoughby, S. S. (2000). Perspectives on mathematics education. In Burke, M. J., & Curcio, F. R. (Eds.). *Learning mathematics for a new century: 2000 yearbook* (pp. 1–15). Reston, VA: National Council of Teachers of Mathematics.

Wisconsin Department of Public Instruction. (2007). *Mathematics: Adolescent learning toolkit.* Madison, WI: Author.

Wolfe, P. (2001). *Brain matters: Translating research into classroom practice.* Alexandria, VA: Association for Supervision and Curriculum Development.

Wu, H. (1999, Fall). Basic skills versus conceptual understanding: A bogus dichotomy in mathematics education. *American Educator,* 1–7.

Ysseldyke, J., & Bolt, D. (2007, September). Effect of technology-enhanced continuous progress monitoring on math achievement. *School Psychology Review, 36*(3), 453–468.

Zemelman, S., Daniels, H., & Hyde, A. (1998). *Best practice: New standards for teaching and learning in America's schools.* Portsmouth, NH: Heinemann.

Contributors to the first edition

Gary Appel
NCREL

Malcolm Butler
SERVE

Anne Collins
Massachusetts, ASSM

Ella-Mae Daniel
SERVE

Elaine DeBassige D'Amato
McREL

Judy Florian
McREL

Fred Gross
TERC

Jodean Grunow
Wisconsin, ASSM

Carol Hanley
Kentucky, CSSS

Clare Heidema
McREL

Bill Hopkins
Texas, ASSM

Deb Jordan
McREL

Mozell Lang
Michigan, CSSS

Arlene Mitchell
McREL

Brett Moulding
Utah, CSSS

Randi Peterson
McREL

Gwen Pollock
Illinois, CSSS

Linda Schoen
South Carolina, CSSS

Sharon Stenglein
Minnesota, ASSM

Jan Tuomi
McREL

Jim Woodland
Nebraska, CSSS

Editors

Jim Harper
RBS

Barbara Hicks
AEL

Nancy Kellogg

Carolyn Richbart

Lynn Richbart

Vicki Urquhart
McREL

Janie Zimmer
RBS

Librarians

Linda Brannan
McREL

Norma Brown
McREL

Terry Young
McREL

Graphics and Layout

Dawn McGill
McREL

Molly Drew
McREL

Indexing

James Sucha
McREL

Index

Notes

Notes

Notes

Notes

Notes

Notes